A History of the Independent Bar of South Australia

Updated Edition

AF896394

Also available from
jjemerson.com

All custom printed with the option of a personalised book plate

Essays in Advocacy
Introduction by the Hon. Robert French AC
edited by Tom Gray, Martin Hinton and David Caruso
Barr Smith Press
9780987171832 | 610 pp

The Crown
Foreword by the Hon. Justice Stephen Gageler AC
edited by Martin Hinton and John M. Williams
University of Adelaide Press
9781925261790 | 394 pp

First Among Equals
Foreword by the Hon. Justice John Doyle AC QC,
Barr Smith Press
by John Emerson
9780863968365 | 290 pp

Hague's History of the Law in South Australia 1837–1867
Foreword by Martin Hinton QC
Barr Smith Press, University of Adelaide
9781925261882 | 956 pp

Available from
Monash University Publishing

John Jefferson Bray: a vigilant life
Foreword by the Hon. Michael Kirby AC CMG
by John Emerson
Monash University Publishing
9781922235619 | 272 pp

A History of the Independent Bar of South Australia

Updated Edition

John Emerson

Original 2006 Foreword
by
Sir Anthony Mason AC KBE

First published in 2006 by
University of Adelaide Barr Smith Press

Updated Edition 2020
© John Emerson 2006, 2020

Original publication of this book was supported by:
Private donors
The John Bray Law Network of the University of Adelaide Alumni Association
Law School, University of Adelaide

The author gratefully acknowledges permission from *The Advertiser* for the use of some photos in the Queen's Counsel part.

All rights reserved. This book is copyright. Apart from any fair dealing for the purposes of private study, research, criticism or review, as permitted under the Copyright Act, no part may be reproduced without written permission. Enquiries should be addressed to the publisher at the email address below.

Hardback ISBN: 978-0-6450056-0-8
Paperback ISBN: 978-0-6450056-1-5

This edition designed and published by
John Emerson Publishing Solutions
web: jjemerson.com
email: john@jjemerson.com

Typeset in Cormorant and Optima
Printed, bound and distributed by Ingram Lightning Source (worldwide locations)

NATIONAL LIBRARY OF AUSTRALIA
A catalogue record for this work is available from the National Library of Australia

Contents

Acknowledgments **VII**

Author's Note **IX**

Original Preface by the Hon. C J Legoe AO QC **XI**

Original Foreword by Sir Anthony Mason AC KBE **XIII**

PART ONE – History and Development

1 Introduction: "The Reluctant Debutante" 3

2 Expansion: From 1964 till 2020 **21**

PART TWO – Bluestone

3 Adelaide Chambers: The Bluestone Phenomenon **47**

PART THREE – Silks

4 Queen's and Senior Counsel Appointments 1974–2020 **139**

Conclusion **271**

Bibliography **273**

Index **277**

Acknowledgments

Over the course of both editions many busy people were kind enough to allow me their time in the form of interviews, photocopying, filling in forms, chasing up all sorts of fragments of information. I am especially grateful to the Clerks of Chambers, who are first reason barristers set up chambers. The University of Adelaide Law School, courtesy of Deans Kath McEvoy and Professor Paul Fairall, more recently Melissa De Zwart, has provided me with ongoing office facilities, and welcomed me into the School's active academic life.

I thank Michael Abbott QC, Sam Abbott, Jane Alexander at Howard Zelling Chambers, Grant Algie QC, Hon. Tim Anderson, Jill Barnes, Michelle Barnes, Michael Barnett, Rosey Boehm, Gordon Barrett QC, Michelle Bele, Michael Birchall, Hon. David Bleby QC, Darren Blight QC, Kevin Borick QC, Geoffrey Britton, Gabby Brown, Tim Bryant, Sally Burgess, Rob Cameron, Ray Choate, Pam Cleland, Anthony Crocker, Sathish Dasan, Meredith Dickson, Di Dawson, Professor Michael Detmold, Hon. John Doyle AC QC, Debbie Duncan, Sophia Edmonds, Scott Evans, Martin Frayne SC, Joana Fuller, Dr Rachael Gray QC, Hon. Tom Gray QC, Kerryn Green (Edmund Barton), Bruce Greenhalgh, David Greenwell, the late Geoffrey Hackett-Jones QC, the late David Haines QC, Sandy Hancock, Andrew Harris QC, Lorna Hartwell, Brian Hayes QC, Scott Henchliffe QC, Henry Heuzenroeder, Paul Heywood-Smith QC, Stephen Hodder, Rachel Hodgson, Veronica Horrocks, Helen Horton, Kate Jennings, the late Hon. Elliott Johnston AM QC, Ed Jolly, Myranwy Kanes, Dr John Keeler, Margaret Kelly, the late Hon. Len King AC QC, Hon. Justice Chris Kourakis (Chief Justice), Hon. Robert Lawson QC, Robyn Layton QC, Patricia Lee, Hon. Christopher Legoe AO QC, Holly Leeson, Stuart Lindsay, David Lovell QC, Neil Lowrie, Michael Magarey, Hon. Sir Anthony Mason AC KBE, Marina Matthews, Dianne Mifsud, the late Hon. Robin Millhouse QC, Sue Milne, Margaret Minney (née Sangster), Stephen Mitchell, late Hon. Bob Mohr, Neville Morcombe QC, the late Hon. Ted Mullighan QC, Peter Norman, Hon. Margaret Nyland AM, Duanne Peck, the late Hon. John Perry AO QC, the late Mark Pickhaver, Lindy Powell QC, Kelvyn Prescott CSM, Nick Ramage, Ranae (Campbell Chambers), Ian Robertson SC, Steve Roder, Anthony Russell QC, Christine Salvemini, Marie Shaw QC, Shane Spence, Greg Stevens, Hon. Justice Steven Strickland, Hon. John Sulan QC, Sydney Tilmouth QC, Andrew Tokley QC, Chris Tonkin, Hon. John von Doussa AO QC, Nickie Waddington, Jonathan Wells QC, Eileen West, Vickianne West and Hon. Tim Williams QC. If I have inadvertently missed someone I apologise.

Author's Note

As someone with degrees in Humanities and none in law, when I began the original research for this book I knew very little about barristers in South Australia. I came to acquire a passionate respect for this relatively small group of self-reliant individuals who have had the confidence to sign the Bar Roll – that is the main criterion for inclusion in this book – and become masters and mistresses of their own destiny.

In historical terms, the South Australian independent bar is quite young – almost all except a half-dozen or so of its entire membership were alive at the time of the 2006 publication, including founder the Honourable Christopher Legoe AO QC. Because of its exponential growth since the 1980s, the majority of those at that time who had signed the bar roll were not only still alive, but either actively in practice or holding a judicial or government office. This meant that rather than consulting musty old documents under the guard of suspicious archivists, I had the pleasure of meeting in person over a hundred present and past members of the independent bar.

My general aim was to produce a social history – that is tracing the independent bar's origins and development as a group. There is almost no discussion of cases or legal matters. I have consciously kept nomenclature simple for ease of flow – except where context specifically demands it. Titles and post-nominals such as "QC", "SC", "Honourable", and so on are only used where necessary, as they can also become quickly outdated.

I have been democratic in my approach to barristers and sets of chambers – giving them the choice of the material they are willing to let me use. This means that in the chapter on the chambers there is much variation on each entry, extent of details and the photos provided. I did not want to fit every set of chambers and every barrister into the same template for the sake of the appearance of the book.

There are over 500 people mentioned in this book who are collectively the source of the majority of the material used in its writing. The bar is still relatively young and little exists by way of publicly available archival sources. Using primarily oral sources increases room for error but is how historical records must start. I have tried to eliminate inaccuracies. If you notice a wrong year, mispelling or inconsistency I apologise and take full responsibility. I also must ask the indulgence for anyone who spies an uncredited photograph – please let me know. The words "current" and "present", for the benefit of future readers, refer to the year 2020.

John Emerson
30 October 2020

Preface to the 2006 edition

Hon. Christopher Legoe AO QC

The idea of writing this book was suggested a few years ago. It is due to the initiative and foresight of the Hon. Justice Tom Gray who engaged Dr John Emerson to write this history of the first fifty years of a specialised branch of the legal profession in South Australia.

John Emerson, a history scholar, has written up the changing structure of legal practice since colonisation here and elsewhere in Australia in a very readable form. His research has revealed important aspects of this change, particularly since the 1950s. He has made many observations relating to the formation and development of an independent group of barristers both experienced and inexperienced when they elected to join the bar. The book demonstrates how all those who made that election over the last fifty years contributed to the status and strength that it currently enjoys. It is their dedication and professional skills that have established and maintained the bar.

Many thanks should be given to all those who have helped and contributed to the preparation and publication of this book. They know who they are and the readers are the beneficiaries. The story and events recorded in this book open the door to memories which may otherwise be closed and forgotten.

Christopher Legoe
The original Reluctant Debutante

Foreword to the 2006 edition

Hon. Sir Anthony Mason AC KBE

The history of the South Australian Bar, as related by John Emerson, is a fascinating story. The record tells us that it began with the courageous decision of Christopher Legoe in 1955 to set himself up in practice solely as a barrister and to seek exemption from the obligation to keep a trust account. This he did with the acquiescence of the Law Society which has, ever since, maintained a friendly relationship with the Bar.

Although Legoe's decision was taken 120 years after the foundation of the colony, his decision reflected what the minuscule legal profession had in mind from the colony's early days - ultimately to divide into the separate branches of solicitors and barristers.

Legoe practised as a barrister in splendid isolation for seven years before he was joined by others. Since then the Bar has continued to grow. Its membership now exceeds 170.

The emergence of a separate Bar has enhanced the quality of advocacy in South Australia, just as it has done in Western Australia. In both States, the majority of judges are now appointed from the ranks of the Bar.

John Emerson's work is much more than a simple history of the Bar The photographs and the short biographical notes bring to life the personalities and the bluestone buildings which house their Chambers. One of the buildings may have been in earlier use by the one profession which can justly claim to have a longer history than the legal profession.

So far, however, the Bar has failed to produce a lawyer to match the dashing skill of South Australia's first judge, John Jeffcott, who, the author tells us, managed to avoid conviction for killing a man in a duel near Exeter and eluded his creditors who were waiting to arrest him when he embarked for South Australia. He drowned in a storm at the mouth of the River Murray in 1837 on his way to visit his fiancée (a cousin) in Tasmania.

John Emerson also provides us with a perceptive account of the condition of the legal system in England at the time of the South Australian settlement and what that meant for the establishment of a legal system in the new colony. In addition, he outlines the legal and political issues which related to the emergence of a separate Bar and the differences between South Australia and the approaches taken in the eastern colonies, particularly New South Wales.

This book is a model history of a profession. For the future it will be a source of continuing interest to the Bar, to the legal profession generally and to all those who are interested in the early history and legal foundations of the Australian colonies.

Anthony Mason
9 February 2006

Part One

History and Development

Chapter One

Introduction
"The Reluctant Debutante"

Around September 1955, Christopher Legoe sent a letter to the President of the Law Society, Frank Piper QC, advising him that he would be setting up practice solely as a barrister and asking for exemption from the requirement to maintain a trust account. Unfortunately for posterity, the letter was not kept, as it represented a major new direction for South Australia's fused legal profession – then almost 120 years old.

The Law Society granted Christopher Legoe the necessary exemption. South Australia's independent bar began one morning two months later, on the 15th of September 1955 when he arrived in his small office in the Epworth Building on Pirie Street. For almost seven years, he was South Australia's only independent barrister in a fused profession, which numbered around 300 in total in the State at that time. Jack Elliott doubled the numbers in 1962, and the profession doubled in size again two years later with the addition of Robin Millhouse and Howard Zelling. That year – 1964 – The South Australian Bar Association was formed, and a roll of barristers created. Until 2020, the number of independent practising barristers in the State has grown to around 230.

The divided English legal profession that South Australia inherited in 1836 had been in varying degrees of conflict between its many branches for centuries. The serjeants, barristers, solicitors, attorneys, proctors, scriveners and a variety of court officials and clerks, all performed functions which overlapped to some degree and there was a push for consolidation. By the 1830s the profession and the multitude of parallel court systems in which it worked had reached a critical point.

The original division between those who pleaded in court and those who completed the background preparation can be traced back as least as far back as Cicero in pro Murena two thousand years ago. The Roman jurist considered the advocate who appeared in court on behalf of others to lead a noble profession, as opposed to the humble status of the mere legal drudge.[1] Twelve hundred years later this division reappeared in England. The Serjeants-at-Law who had the exclusive right of audience in the Court of Common Pleas located at Westminster in London kept apprentices. Some of these apprentices chose to become advocates in the Exchequer courts and the peripatetic King's or Queen's Bench, and the others chose to become attorneys doing the preparatory work.[2]

Those apprentices who chose the path of advocacy formed into a new branch and based themselves in London, forming inns from which to work, live and educate in turn. Four of these inns survived the mediaeval period in which they were founded: Inner Temple, Middle Temple, Lincoln's Inn and Gray's Inn. An important part of the education was the mock trial, or moot. Students were separated from practising advocates by a bar in the mock court room. When they had competently completed their education the students were called to this bar, and from 1590 this calling to the bar became the judicially recognised sign of having legal learning.[3] There was also another bar in the courts which separated the judge from the prisoner in the dock and from the rest of the courtroom. From as early as the fourteenth century the word 'bar' came to mean 'court', but by the end of the seventeenth century, it was also being used to mean the barristers as a professional group.[4]

Solicitors emerged in competition with the attorneys in the first part of the sixteenth century, concentrated in the Chancery Courts. They were not formally enrolled as officers of the court as were the attorneys, and the lack of need for either qualifications or registration unfortunately attracted some unscrupulous individuals. Attorneys, solicitors and scriveners made most of their money from land transactions – conveyances. They also began handling the preliminaries to litigation, and by the middle of the eighteenth century it had become standard practice for clients planning litigation to approach attorneys and solicitors who would then approach a barrister.

But the attorneys and solicitors began to try and prevent all direct client contact with barristers as this would give them power over the bar, and compensate them for not being able to appear in the superior courts themselves. As a result, young barristers in the latter part of the 1700s increasingly found that if they did not win the favour of attorneys, they would not establish their career. The Society of Gentlemen Practisers, which attorneys and solicitors formed in 1729, made a show of its power in 1766 when it banned Serjeant Davy from being employed as a Counsel for referring to the "ignorance of attorneys".[5] He had to apologise publicly to win back their business. The Society continued its push to prevent litigants from accessing barristers directly, but the Inns of Court defended its ancient practice of its members receiving briefs directly, and it was only well after the settling of South Australia – at the very beginning of the twentieth century – that they began accepting briefs only from solicitors. Barristers also until this time continued to do conveyances.

By the 1830s, the English legal professions were by no means clearly divided into two branches, although there was a clear division between those who were members of the Inns of Court and those who were not. The decades either side of South Australia's settlement were decades of much reform in England's legal constitution. Writers and philosophers such as Jeremy Bentham, John Stuart Mill, Robert Owen, Thomas Arnold, Thomas Carlyle, Charles Dickens and Mrs Gaskell were appalled at the quality of life for most English people, and were writing books and pamphlets calling for changes.[6]

Key reforms include the abolition in 1817 of the public whipping of women, in 1833 of slavery throughout the British Empire and the reduction of the working hours of children.[7] The number of crimes for which hanging was the penalty was reduced from 200 in 1826 to four in 1861. The pillory (stocks) was abolished in 1837, transportation for simple larceny in 1849, transportation for larceny in 1849, and most corporal punishment in 1861.[8] There was an important reform in 1836 when people charged with felony were allowed to have defence counsel for the whole of their case rather than just for legal argument and cross-examinations. The Old Bailey, specialising in criminal trials, opened in 1834.

But the courts at this time were still in an appalling situation. Legacees were waiting up to twenty years for the Chancery Court – the court which dealt exclusively with equity cases – to settle an estate because of Lord Eldon's obsessive perfectionism.[9] A common problem encountered by suitors was that the various courts had no clearly defined limits to their jurisdictions. A litigant could pursue his case through to the House of Lords only to discover that he had from the first step chosen the wrong court.[10] The second major problem was that the courts administered, in Holdsworth's words, "systems of law which were not merely rival, but even directly contradictory".[11] In 1768 Blackstone in his *Commentaries III* noted that "in a single instance two different rules of property [clashed] with or [contradicted] each other", and in 1834 the situation had not changed. Palgrave noted how the same case that could obtain a decree in a common law court would fail in an equity one.[12]

Two events would sound the death knoll finally on the old courts system and allow the reforms of the following fifty years: the resignation of Lord Eldon as Lord Chancellor in 1827 and his successor Lord Brougham's six- hour speech to the House of Commons in 1828 detailing the deficiencies of the courts and the remedies needed to fix them. Brougham did more than just make that speech, he set the wheels of reform in motion.

But the colonies were saved from the confusion caused by the multiple, overlapping courts, simply because they did not have the population to support them. In South Australia the Supreme Court Act united all the courts into one on day one – which remains the case today. South Australian litigants were thus spared from the start from the interlacing maze of the Courts of Common Pleas, King's Bench, Exchequer, Chancery, Ecclesiastical and Admiralty. The first judge of the South Australian Supreme Court, Sir John Jeffcott (1796–1837) also saved the State from the ongoing rivalries of the English legal profession by admitting the first lawyer, Charles Mann (Snr) as a barrister, solicitor, attorney and proctor. All lawyers since in South Australia have been admitted as such. England would have to wait until 1873 to establish a single Supreme Court and create the modern division of its legal profession into the two branches of barristers and solicitors.[13]

Sir John Forbes had already given New South Wales the single Supreme Court that England would have to wait fifty years for in 1824.[14] But the notion of a fused profession was anathema to two English barristers, William Wentworth (1792–1872) and Robert Wardell (1794–1834). They arrived in Sydney in September 1824, just four months after the first sitting of the first Supreme Court in Australia. After being admitted they immediately sought an order for the division of the profession.[15] Chief Justice Forbes dismissed the motion as he did not believe that Sydney was capable of supporting a division. Wentworth and Wardell pushed for division and it was eventually made legislation in 1835, although Wardell did not live to see it, being killed by an escaped convict the year before.

Sydney at this time only had a population of 70,000, which included 20,000 convicts. There were three judges of the Supreme Court and around 40 lawyers.[16] But New South Wales at this time included not only the whole of the eastern part of Australia, but also the Northern Territory and part of Western Australia, completely enveloping South Australia until 1857.

Victoria and Queensland were still districts under ultimate rule from Sydney. Thus Melbourne was given a divided profession in 1841 when its branch of the Supreme Court opened, with a population of just 4,500.[17] Brisbane got a resident judge in 1856, three years before it became a State in its own right. To this day Queensland and New South Wales are the only two States or territories in Australia to have a legal profession officially divided by Statute. Victoria fused the profession officially in 1891, although in practice the vast majority of the legal profession there practise as if there was a formal division.

The first meeting in South Australia to discuss division of the legal profession took place barely five years after settlement, in August 1841. Twenty-one practitioners were present at the meeting, which must have been more or less the entire profession at that time. Six members declared their desire to be barristers: Smillie (Advocate-General), Mann, Fisher, Nicholls, George Morphett and Poulden.[18] But unlike Wentworth and Wardell in New South Wales, none of these men were trained as barristers at the Inns of Court. There were only two who were – Henry Jickling and Nicholls. Justice Cooper – sole judge at that time – was not convinced that division was appropriate yet.

The desire for division remained strong however, and Advocate-General (old title for Attorney-General) Smillie strongly believed that it had proved convenient in England.[19] As a result, Ordinance 6 of the Supreme Court Act of 1845 gave the judges of the Supreme Court of South Australia the power to divide the legal profession at any future time they believed appropriate.

The last most notable debate in the nineteenth century over the division of the profession resulted from the first three Queen's Counsel appointments in 1865. These were Randolph Stow, R B Andrews and W A Wearing. The only one of these who conformed strictly to the English tradition of appointees to silk was Wearing, who had been admitted to Lincoln's Inn in 1841.[20] Andrews had been an attorney of Queen's Bench and a Chancery Court solicitor. Randolph Stow had completed articles in Adelaide and so was, in purist eyes, no better than a solicitor either. Justice Benjamin Boothby was horrified at this tampering with the long-standing tradition of appointing barristers, and only barristers to the office:

> This union of the office of Queen's Counsel with that of practising attorney has, I apprehend, never before been known of in any Court of Her Majesty where only the law and practice of the Superior Courts at Westminster is administered.[21]

Traditionalists must have continued to question the practice of appointing non-barristers to silk for many more years, as the South Australian government in 1912 replaced the word "barrister" with "practitioner" so that it read: "no practitioner of the Supreme Court shall be appointed Her Majesty's Counsel except on the recommendation of the Chief Justice".[22] But strictly speaking there was no need at all for the change in wording, since all lawyers admitted to practice in South Australia were admitted, among the other offices, as barristers.

The replacement of "barrister' with "practitioner" does, however, reveal the change that had taken place in the South Australian legal profession towards an eventual division. This change in wording shows that an "amalgam" barrister and solicitor of the fused profession was officially recognised as having equal status as a barrister elsewhere who was eligible for appointment to silk. In other words, the fused profession in South Australia was effectively giving itself the same credibility and recognition as the separate bars. This is certainly justifiable in the light of two Chief Justices who excelled – Sir Richard Hanson had proven a brilliant jurist and Sir Samuel Way a brilliant judge. Neither was a barrister in the strictest sense of the term. Hanson had been an English attorney and Way did articles in Adelaide – the only local form of legal training available – which in England would have qualified him only as a solicitor.

By 1928 the fused profession was established and accepted in South Australia. The topic of division was again in the air and the judges of the Supreme Court invited the Law Society of South Australia to conduct a plebiscite to ascertain the level of support.[23] In fact, less than one quarter of the three hundred members of the profession who voted desired division.[24] As it turned out, 64 voted 'Yes' and 209 voted 'No': an overwhelming 76.6 per cent. One of the possible reasons for this change of sentiment may have been that firms by this time had adapted very well to financial benefits of briefing their own in-house Counsel, with an additional drawcard if any of them were King's Counsel.

Nevertheless, it was long recognised that the more time practitioners could spend in court, the better they became at it. It was also a fact that appearing in court was not compatible with being available in an office for clients. Standard practice in Adelaide legal firms evolved to allow for one partner to concentrate on advocacy and another to stay present in the office and attend to the rest of legal work. This was how Chief Justices such as Way, Murray, Napier, Bray and King were able to gain their reputations as exceptional barristers. Even in Samuel Way's tiny practice with only one other partner – James Brook – Way did the court work and Brook the solicitor's work. Similarly, George Murray specialised as Counsel while his partner W A Magarey was the solicitor. Jack Elliott tells us in *Memoirs of a Barrister* of how he became the barrister in the firm, while his brother Don was the solicitor. Len King, who was establishing his career around the time Christopher Legoe was in the Crown Law Office, took on a partner in order to concentrate on the barristerial work.

Less recognised still was the lack of independence of even those members of a firm who did specialise in advocacy, but who could never give opinions or represent clients from other firms. Around a hundred years after the founding of the fused profession in South Australia, there was a sign of change. Geoffrey Reed had been filling in as an Acting Justice from April 1935 to July 1937 during the absences of firstly, Chief Justice Sir George Murray, and then Justice Mellis Napier. Prior to filling in on the bench, he had mainly practised as a solicitor, and he must have noticed while sitting on the cases before him how much more efficiently they were conducted by those lawyers who concentrated on court work.[25] In that mid-1930s period the leading Counsel included Crown Prosecutor Roderick Chamberlain, Frank Villeneuve Smith KC, E E Cleland KC, and Joe Nelligan.[26] A month after stepping back down from the bench in July 1937, Geoffrey Reed was appointed King's Counsel. He decided to practise from then on independently as a barrister, and he set up chambers in the Bowman Buildings in King William Street.[27]

In July 1943, Geoffrey Reed was appointed to the Supreme Court permanently after the death of Justice E E Cleland.[28] This first spark that might have begun a separate bar in South Australia appeared to have been extinguished. But this was happily not the case at all. In February 1953, the year he was knighted, Geoffrey Reed appointed Christopher John Legoe as his Associate, just returned from his education in England.

Christopher Legoe had been in Cambridge studying law and was a student at the Inner Temple in London, where he was called to the bar in October 1951. He had then spent a year in pupillage with Colin Duncan, who specialised in defamation cases. Colin Duncan published with Brian Neill the seminal work, Defamation, which came out in a second edition in 1983 as Duncan and Neill on Defamation.[29] Christopher Legoe spent one year with

Sir Geoffrey Reed, and during this time they discussed the potential for a separate bar operating within the South Australian legal profession.

In March 1954, Christopher Legoe went to work for the Crown Law Office, and began to gain his first direct experiences in advocacy. During this period he realised that he wanted to practise as a barrister in South Australia, and he did not see the point in view of this aim of also having to do solicitors' work. The traditional method of entering the profession in South Australia was to be articled to a lawyer in a similar way to how solicitors were in New South Wales and England, while completing a Bachelor of Laws at the University of Adelaide. After qualifying, the new lawyers spent their early careers doing solicitors' work and gradually made appearances in court. Only later, were those who proved talented in carrying out the firm's advocacy work able to specialise in it.

But unlike the South Australian trained lawyers, Christopher Legoe had trained specifically as a barrister in England and knew little about the work that solicitors did. His situation was therefore quite different. After about fifteen months working in the Crown Law Office, he took a month's leave and went up to his family's pastoral property in the Pilbara region of Western Australia. He needed to make his mind up about if and how he might realistically pursue a career as an independent barrister in South Australia. Would he get any work? What would be the reaction of the established legal profession? He had the advantage of coming from a family which had generated a large fortune in developing South Australia. His great-great uncle was Sir Thomas Elder (1818–1897), who with his brothers opened up great areas of pastoral land and provided the venture capital for the Wallaroo and Moonta copper mines. Sir Thomas was also one of the original major benefactors of the University of Adelaide, followed by his brother-in-law Robert Barr Smith (1824-1915) and nephew, Tom Elder Barr Smith (1863–1941) – Christopher Legoe's great grandfather and grandfather respectively.[30]

Encouraged by Sir Geoffrey Reed and Law Society President, Frank Piper QC, Christopher Legoe began practising as a barrister a little while after he returned from the Pilbara. He was just 27 years old. The first firms and lawyers that sent him briefs include Fisher Jeffries, Murray & Cudmore, Norman Waterhouse & Mutton, Bob Fisher, Don Brebner, Maurice and David Bednall, and Jack Cornish. These practices quickly realised the advantage of briefing out to a specialist who freed them from appearing in court without risk of losing the client. Another source of briefs was former employer, the Crown Solicitor, who from time to time made use of Chris Legoe's availability to prosecute when their staff were already committed elsewhere.

Most of the briefs were for civil matters. Legoe's first appearance in the South Australian law reports is in 1957 for one of the Crown briefs: Queen v Todd.[31] This was a reference in the Full Court on the question of whether "effecting a public mischief" was an indictable offence in South Australia. Although the court answered in the negative, the judgment notes that the matter was "ably and fully argued by Mr Legoe".[32]

Christopher Legoe around 1952. (CJL)

The Supreme Court bench in 1957 had been presided over for fifteen years by Sir Mellis Napier. The other judges were Sir Herbert Mayo, Sir Geoffrey Reed, Sir George Ligertwood, Charles Abbott and Bruce Ross. The Crown Solicitor was Roderic Chamberlain who had been in the Crown Law Department since 1926. The silks who led the bar then included Harry Alderman, John Bray, Frank Piper, Joe Nelligan, V R Millhouse and A L Pickering. Other names appearing regularly in the reports include Andrew Wells, J R Kearnan, D R Newman, Rod Matheson, Sam Jacobs, J H Bagot, C Villeneuve Smith, Bob Fisher, Len King and Don Dunstan. Firmly in charge of South Australia was Sir Thomas Playford who had been premier since 1938.

Although Christopher Legoe was doing what the legal profession had intended to do from the moment of its establishment in South Australia – eventually divide along the lines of the English profession – there was nevertheless a measure of mixed feelings about the impact a potential separate bar may have on the existing legal profession. Some established firms and their senior practitioners were concerned that their lifetime's work was threatened. Others supported Legoe's example, although no one yet followed it. On 29 September 1959 the Law Society of South Australia held the annual general meeting at Rechabite Hall in Victoria Square. After the meeting, President David Hogarth invited E W Palmer to open a general discussion on the division of the profession.

A heated and passionate argument took place into the night. Some senior practitioners such as R N Irwin and J F Brazel spoke vehemently against division, arguing that the profession was not big enough to support it. Others such as L J Elliott argued equally vehemently in favour.[33] Chris Legoe felt that as the young sole barrister in company with so many senior practitioners he would keep quiet. The minutes book records some of those who spoke, but not in this meeting, their position: C T Hargrave, A K Sangster, D R Newman, L J Elliott, E E McLoughlin, R M Duffy, G H McCarthy, J L Travers QC, A L Pickering QC, F B Moran, E L Stevens, J F Brazel QC, J J Redman and C Sandery. The minutes discreetly end:

> At 10.50 pm other members still wished to speak (...). It was resolved that no statement as to the discussion be given to the press. The meeting closed at 11.00 pm. Signed, David Hogarth.

Another meeting was held in the Rechabite Hall two months later – on Monday, 30 November 1959 at 8 pm to discuss whether any division of the legal profession should be voluntary, as in Victoria, or compulsory as in New South Wales and England. Around 160 members of the legal profession were present. This time the minutes record those who spoke in favour:

> Messrs N.J.W. Birchall, L.J.Elliott, G.J.Joseph, R.N. Matulich, C.W. Villeneuve Smith, H.E. Zelling, M.W. Bednall, L.M.S. Hargrave, R.D. Elliott, C.H. Bright, F.B. Moran, E.E. McLaughlin, E.F. Johnston, J.J. Redman and J.D. O'Sullivan.

and those who spoke against:

> Messrs J.N. McEwin, M.L.W. Bevan, J.H. Muirhead, J.C.E. McCarthy, A.L Pickering QC, D.A. Abbott, R.N. Irwin, N.C. Ligertwood, A.W. Cocks, F.L Field, Dr J.J. Bray QC, Messrs H.G. Alderman, C.A.L. Abbott and G.C. Harry.[34]

The meeting agreed to conduct a secret ballot among the members of the Law Society of South Australia and ascertain firstly, whether or not they are in favour of division of the profession into barristers and solicitors. The result for this question was 76 for and 154 against. The second question asked that in the event of division would they favour a voluntary division (as in Victoria) or compulsory division (as in New South Wales). The result to this question was 139 for a voluntary division and 87 for a compulsory one.

During this latter part of 1959, Chris Legoe had also been involved in one of the most important briefs of his early career: the Stuart Royal Commission.[35] Legoe was junior counsel to J F Brazel QC, assisting the

Commission, which sat from Monday, 17 August until 26 October. It gave its report on the 3 December, just a few days after the final general meeting over the division of the legal profession. The Stuart Royal Commission also led to a defamation case against News editor Rohan Rivett, who was charged formally in January 1960 for headlines and banners published in August 1959. The Royal Commission took place largely because of political pressure resulting from the campaign led by the News, which Rupert Murdoch then owned and managed directly in Adelaide. Debate has continued to this day as to the impact that the Stuart Affair had on the South Australian legal and political systems, but if nothing else, it is probably the first example of media intervention in these processes.

Because of the results of the secret ballot indicating that the majority of the legal profession did not want change, the Law Society of South Australia did not hold any more meetings or take any more action. This left the profession the freedom to develop itself in the organic way that it has. Instead of having to conform to a formalised structure, the profession now had the flexibility to respond to the needs of the South Australian community. This is possibly the most important characteristic of the independent bar in South Australia, as it only grew because it fulfilled a need, not because people were obliged to use it as in New South Wales and England.

Lionel John (Jack) Elliott QC (1914–2001). (Supreme Court Library of South Australia)

Although Christopher Legoe's specialisation in advocacy quickly showed its benefits not just to the litigants, but to the judicial process itself, his example was not followed by even the most passionate of his supporters, Jack Elliott, until August 1962. This is why he calls the independent bar in south Australia "the reluctant debutante". But the open discussions in 1959 nevertheless had the effect of inspiring some of the other practitioners in favour of a specialist bar eventually to take the plunge. By the time Jack Elliott had set up chambers in Gouger Street, Chris Legoe had moved from the Epworth

Building and was practising from Cowra Chambers at 23 Grenfell Street – since demolished to make way for the 25-storey tower which, with other tenants, was the seat of the Federal Court in South Australia until 2005.

Jack Elliot was appointed Queen's Counsel in 1962. Howard Zelling was also appointed silk that year and in May 1964, he became the third barrister, setting up chambers in Wright Street. At the end of 1963, Robin Millhouse sat by chance at a Law Society dinner next to Chris Legoe, whom he had first met in 1947 just before Legoe went to Cambridge. Robin Millhouse was unhappy at the firm Baker McEwin Millhouse & Co. and his father – the Honourable Justice Vivian Millhouse – had just died at 61 years of age. Millhouse was too young to have the reputation of senior practitioners such as Jack Elliott and Howard Zelling that would guarantee briefs, but he had been the State member for the electorate of Mitcham since 1955. This gave him a regular income as a backup. In addition, Parliament then only sat on Tuesday, Wednesday and Thursday afternoons. He accepted Chris Legoe's invitation to join him at Cowra Chambers and became the State's fourth barrister in July 1964. Briefs came in for him, but never from Baker McEwin.

Hon. Robin Rhodes Millhouse QC (1929–2017). (Law Society of SA)

With four committed barristers now in Adelaide, one could claim that there was now unofficially a "separate" bar – in the collective sense. Acceptance of the existence and usefulness of a separate bar in the State was growing quickly but many years later Chris Legoe admitted:

> (...) we found that the attitude of a large section of the profession was not only sceptical about our choice of practising but at times critical and even somewhat obstructive.[36]

Opposition came not just from with South Australia, where the principal objection was the perceived extra cost of briefing out, but also from interstate, whose long established divided professions – formal or defacto – were reluctant to accept the new South Australian barristers on equal terms.

The logical step in any case was to formalise the new bar and the inaugural meeting of the South Australian Bar Association was held in Howard Zelling's chambers on 23 December 1964. A humble exercise book was pronounced the Roll and all four barristers signed it, with the undertaking:

> Every person subscribing to this Roll undertakes to practise exclusively as Counsel, to abide by all the rulings of the South Australian Bar Council and to pay the annual subscription required by the Council.

Hon. Howard Edgar Zelling QC (1916–2000). (Supreme Court Library of South Australia)

That exercise book has continued to serve as the official bar roll and crossed 400 signatures in 2014.

This was an era of important development elsewhere in Australia. Perth was a city of more or less the same age and size as Adelaide and in 1961, Francis Burt QC indicated that he would begin practising as a barrister on his own account. He had been a partner in Muir and Williams, and with their support he rented an office from them. Terry Walsh followed his example around the same time, and John Wickham QC brought the number of independent barristers in Western Australia to three in June 1962. All of them leased some more rooms from Muir and Williams and formed the first set of barristers' chambers. Gresley Clarkson took the fourth room and in September 1963, they established the Western Australian Bar Association.

Francis Burt invited Chris Legoe to Perth a little bit after this for mutual assistance in resolving the problems of establishing a separate bar in their respective fused professions. This was the start of a lifetime friendship. Both Francis Burt and John Wickham were appointed to the WA Supreme Court bench in 1969. Sir Francis Burt, as he was from 1977, went on to become Chief Justice from 1977 to 1988, and he was the State's governor from 1990 until 1993. John Wickham was also the founding Chancellor of Murdoch University from 1974 until 1980. Of the other two founding Western Australian barristers, Gresley Clarkson was a judge of the Supreme Court in Papua New Guinea (1966–1975) and Terence Walsh – by far the youngest of the four – was a justice of the WA Supreme Court from 1988–1998 and Chair of the Parole Board.

While the fledgling South Australian and Western Australian bars were establishing themselves, the Australian Bar Association was being founded over in New South Wales. The idea for a national bar association was first suggested in June 1957 at a meeting of the New South Wales Bar Council. It was unhappy that it was not recognised by the Law Council of Australia. Initially the Bar Association of Queensland also supported the idea, but not the Victorians. By 1962, they had changed their minds and on 24

Supreme Court of South Australia bench around the beginning of the 1960s. L-R: Frank Piper, George Ligertwood, Herbert Mayo, Mellis Napier (Chief Justice), Geoffrey Reed, Bruce Ross. (Supreme Court Library of South Australia)

January 1963, the first general meeting of the Australian Bar Association was held in Hobart during the Thirteenth Legal Convention of the Law Council of Australia.[37]

The Australian Bar Association was therefore initially made up of the three eastern States. The South Australian and Western Australian Bar Associations became members in 1968 although Chris Legoe and Terry Walsh had been correspondents for the Australian Bar Gazette since 1964. By 1970 the Australian Capital Territory had also joined, and the Northern Territory Bar would join a few years later – after 1974.

In South Australia Chris Legoe and Howard Zelling began to look for a building that would be suitable for a set of barristers' chambers. Howard Zelling already had his little bluestone cottage in Wright Street, but there was not enough room for anyone else. Nevertheless – and no doubt quite unwittingly – Howard Zelling's choice of chambers began the tradition in South Australia for sets of chambers to tend to be established as a small group in a bluestone heritage building in the streets surrounding the courts. This was a different geographical area from the firms of amalgams, who up till this time clustered in and around the northern end of King William Street.

The search ended in late 1964 when a real estate agent suggested a hundred-year-old double-storey bluestone building at 34 Carrington Street. After the departure of the former occupants – who according to rumour had been in a profession much older than the legal one – the building needed some serious renovating, but was otherwise ideal. Chris Legoe put up fifty per cent, Howard and Sesca Zelling the other, and a new era was ready to begin.

Endnotes

1 Marcus Tullius Cicero (106 BC–43 BC). pro Murena, (63 BC) Capp. IV.
2 Bernard W. Kelly. *A Short History of the English Bar*. London: George Allen, 1908.
3 Wilfrid Prest. "The English Bar, 1550–1700." In Wilfrid Prest (ed.). *Lawyers in Early Modern Europe and America*. London: Croom Helm, 1981, p. 65.
4 Ibid.
5 Brian Abel-Smith and Robert Stevens. *Lawyers and the Courts*. London: Heinemann, 1967, p. 21, fn. 3.
6 Goldwin Smith. *A Constitutional and Legal History of England*. New York: Dorset Press, 1990, p. 444.
7 Ibid., p. 445.
8 Abel-Smith and Stevens, op. cit., pp. 29-30.
9 Ibid., p. 37.
10 Sir William Holdsworth. *A History of English Law*. London: Methuen and Sweet & Maxwell, 1966. Seventh Edition, Vol. 1, p. 634.
11 Ibid., pp. 634-635.
12 Ibid.
13 *The Judicature Act* of 1873. See Abel-Smith and Stevens, pp. 48-50 for a summary.
14 J.M. Bennett. *Sir Francis Forbes*. Leichardt (NSW), Federation Press, 2001, pp. 58-59.
15 J.R.S.Forbes. *The Divided Legal Profession in Australia*. Sydney: The Law Book Company, 1979, p. 36.
16 Ibid., p. 31.
17 Ibid., p. 74.
18 R.M. Hague. *Hague's History of the Law in South Australia, 1837-1867*. Adelaide: University of Adelaide Barr Smith Press, 2005, pp. 729-730.
19 Ibid., p. 170.
20 Graham Loughlin. South Australian Queen's Counsel, 1865-1972. Honours Thesis, University of Adelaide, 1974, p. A127.
21 Ibid., p. 31.
22 Ibid., p. 32.
23 See (1928) 2 ALJ at 13 and at 43.
24 Graham Loughlin, op. cit., p. 33.
25 Ibid., p. A102-103.
26 See Jack Elliott. *Memoirs of a Barrister*. Adelaide: Wakefield Press, 2000, Chapter One. E E Cleland was appointed to the Supreme Court in 1936. Joe Nelligan was appointed KC in 1947.
27 Now demolished. The Bowman Buildings were about 30 metres south of Gilbert Place.
28 Sir Geoffrey Reed was also a returned soldier from World War One, on the Law Society of South Australia Council, a lecturer at the University of Adelaide, one time Acting Dean of the University's Law School and one of the first State editors of *The Australian Law Journal*. See (1943) 17 ALJ 123.

29 London: Butterworths.

30 See Ken Preiss & Pamela Osborn. *The Torrens Park Estate*. Adelaide: Published by the authors, 1991, pp. 59-66.

31 [1957] SASR 305.

32 Ibid., at 307.

33 See Jack Elliott, op. cit., pp. 208-209.

34 Minutes, Law Society of South Australia, 1959.

35 The Stuart Affair remains one of the best known criminal cases in South Australia. It was the subject of three books – by Ken Inglis, *The Stuart Case* in 1961 and a second edition in 2002; Sir Roderic Chamberlain, *The Stuart Affair*, in 1973; and Father Thomas Dixon, *The Wizard of Alice*, in 1987. It was also the subject of the film *Black and White*, released in 2001.

36 Speech at Bar Chambers, ca 1994.

37 See Justice G. Hart and John Helman. "The Founding of the Australian Bar Association". *Australian Bar Gazette*. Vol. 2, October 1968, No. 3, pp. 3-7.

Chapter Two

Expansion
From 1964 till 2020

Bar Chambers had been occupied by the same tenant – Miss E G Bartsch – since 1924. In the Sands & McDougall Adelaide directories the address is listed as a boarding house. The Legoe-Zelling syndicate purchased the house for 10,500 pounds in December 1964, and took possession in February 1965.

The house needed some work on the plumbing and repairs as a result of damage from white ants. It also needed work to transform it into a set of chambers, but Chris Legoe and Robin Millhouse were able to move from Cowra Chambers at 23 Grenfell Street around May 1965. Howard Zelling remained at 24 Wright Street, but nevertheless parked his car behind Bar Chambers. Michael Detmold and Keith Sangster QC moved in later in the year.

The fledgling South Australian bar now had a dedicated set of chambers, which has also been the seat of the South Australian Bar Association. A builder, R G Emery, was appointed to transform and improve the remainder of the property. An extra room was quickly occupied by Robert Mohr, and Michael Birchall took Michael Detmold's place when he became a full-time academic in 1967.

Elsewhere, Jack Elliott was working from his own independent chambers in Gouger Street, and, Howard Zelling remained at 24 Wright Street. He did not wish to move into Bar Chambers immediately, as the Courts Department was going to compulsorily purchase the property for the new District Criminal Courts jurisdiction. Compensation for disrupting his business would be added to the purchase price if he stayed. (As it turned out, around the time the Courts Department bought 24 Wright Street, Howard Zelling was appointed to the Supreme Court. Also, the new District Criminal Court only ever used the old cottage it bought from Howard Zelling as part of its temporary accommodation until moving into the Sir Samuel Way building in 1983.

At the beginning of 1970 the independent bar in South Australia numbered ten members in a total legal profession of around 500 practitioners. Howard Zelling had already been permanently appointed a judge of the Supreme Court in October the year before. By the end of 1970 both Andrew Wells and Keith Sangster had been appointed to the Supreme Court, and Robert Mohr to the new District Criminal Court. Other practitioners took their places, such as Brendan Burns, Frank Boylan, Michael Noblett and Andrew Hodge.

The services of this pioneering group of barristers appealed to solicitors either practising solely or in small partnerships. The difficulty for these practitioners was being absent from the office during the day while attending court. The risk in briefing out to an "in-house counsel" – a member of a firm who effectively only practised as a barrister – was that the counsel's firm then had the opportunity to keep the client. The independent barrister had no such interest in keeping the client once their court business was settled. The solicitor could then remain in his office, remaining available to clients.

The other important factor which would contribute to the successful establishment of the independent bar was that the concentrated practice as an advocate allowed increased experience in advocacy skills. The barristers were specialists, the "amalgams" of the traditional fused profession were generalists. Historically this had not mattered so much but there was at this time a revolution taking place in the legislative arena. The Dunstan government was pushing through major reforms to civil and criminal law, consumer protection and equal opportunities legislation in quantities never seen before. Increasingly complex forensic evidence in criminal trials would also change their nature. The transcript for the trial in 1964 of the last murderer hanged in South Australia was 152 pages. By 1974 the van Beelen trials had produced several thousand.

The combination of convenience, increased quality of advocacy, plethora of new legislation and the subsequent increasing complexity of trials meant that demand for specialist barristers would increase. Resistance nevertheless remained strong from the older members of the profession who had built up firms which offered a complete legal service to their clients, including the prestige for many of access to a resident Queen's Counsel. But some senior partners such as Elliott Johnston, co-founder of Johnston Withers, although never joining the independent bar supported it by sending briefs.

In 1973 Libra Chambers opened on Waterfall Gully Road with Pam Cleland and Kevin Borick. Cleland had been running a firm next door at number 27 since 1964. Libra Chambers only closed in 2002 when Kevin Borick and Sue Davies decided to move into the city. Around the time Pam Cleland retired in 1993 the name changed to Cleland Chambers. As a measure of the success of Cleland's unique choice to found two legal practices in the eastern foothills, former member Margaret Nyland was appointed a judge to the District Court in 1987, then to the Supreme Court in 1993, and David Haines and Kevin Borick were appointed silk in 1999.

In 1975 Bar Chambers added six more chambers bringing the total to fourteen. Over the course of the year David Angel, Andrew Martin, Sydney Tilmouth, Geoffrey Noble, Rob Cameron and David Bright boosted the total number of independent barristers in Adelaide to twenty. Two years later, in 1977, the second city set of chambers opened at 56 Carrington Street, with Tim Anderson, John Doyle and David Quick.

The fact that there were now three separate sets of chambers showed a clear difference in the direction the composition of the independent bar was taking in relation to its twin in Western Australia. The original chambers founded by Francis Burt and John Wickham in 1962 (originally called Bar Chambers and then Francis Burt Chambers) continually expanded and by 2000 housed almost 100 of the state's 160 barristers. On the other hand Bar Chambers in South Australia by 2000 housed no more than ten per cent of the 170 or so members of the independent bar.

Hanson Chambers, as 56 Carrington Street was eventually known, confirmed the tradition that the South Australian bar would develop as a series of small enclaves, more often than not in old, bluestone buildings dating back to the nineteenth century. This development distinguishes South Australia from all the other states and is discussed further in the chapter on chambers.

But the independent bar in Western Australia received crucial support from the judiciary earlier than in South Australia. In 1969 Francis Burt and John Wickham were both appointed to the Western Australian Supreme Court, but even before then, Chief Justice Sir Albert Wolff was a strong supporter of the independent bar. He obliged all new appointees to silk to undertake to join it. In South Australia, neither Sir Mellis Napier nor John Bray offered any support at all. Bray, in fact, was one of those at the Law Society meeting in 1959 who spoke against any division of the legal profession.

Bray's early retirement as Chief Justice in 1978 was certainly a loss for the South Australian Supreme Court, but providential for the immediate viability of the bar. The new Chief Justice, Len King, was a fervent believer in its merits and in 1979, he advised the President of the Law Society that all future appointees to silk would have to sign the following:

> I ... undertake that if I am appointed one of Her Majesty's Counsel I will thereafter confine myself professionally to the proper work of a Queen's Counsel, and observe the professional etiquette appropriate to practice as Queen's Counsel. I understand that this undertaking entails that I cannot practise in partnership or similar association with a solicitor and that I must discontinue as soon as reasonable practicable any such existing partnership or association.

King had always supported the idea of an independent bar. After being appointed to the Supreme Court in 1975, he quickly appreciated the advocacy skills of the specialist barristers who appeared before him in comparison to their amalgam colleagues. He was determined that a Queen's Counsel should be available to take briefs from all sections of the public and the profession free of any obligations to a firm.

The immediate consequence of this requirement was that over the long term firms would no longer be able to use resident Queen's Counsel as a drawcard. Since all new Queen's Counsel would join the independent bar, as the new seat of the best advocates, its reputation began to gain momentum. The table of Queen's Counsel in order of appointment shows the immediate result of Chief Justice King's requirement. Kevin Duggan and John Perry were both appointed in 1979 while practising as counsel within firms and joined the independent bar in 1980, in Bar Chambers.

What is more striking is that the other two appointees to silk that same year – Robin Millhouse and – were already part of the independent bar. In other words, two appointees from the wider profession, which now numbered around 1000, and two from the independent bar, which numbered around 30. The proportions speak for themselves. An examination of the table "Queen's Counsel in order of appointment" shows that from 1984, the appointees were already almost exclusively members of the independent bar, or employed as counsel by the government. Two rare exception of members of firms being appointed after then were John Sulan, in 1990, who joined the bar the year after, and David Wicks, in 1991, who joined the bar in 1992. Therefore, although there has never been any formal requirement for applicants for silk to be already practising independently as barristers, it was recognised very early that the best chance at getting the skills and reputation necessary was to join the bar.

By 1980 the legal profession had doubled in size in just ten years. This meant effectively that half the lawyers had been in practice for less than ten years. So not only were there more lawyers to send briefs to the barristers, but half of the profession had come into it after the establishment of the independent bar. It would take another 17 years for the profession as a whole to double again in size. The independent bar doubled in size to around 60 by 1986, and doubled again from that to around 120 by 1992. By the time the total legal profession crossed the 2000 mark around the year 2000, the independent bar since 1980 had increased in size by a factor of eight to around 160, and was still growing.

Sets of chambers continued to open – Jeffcott in 1982, Murray, Wellington and Campbell in 1984, Rose Park in 1985. Another sign of the increasing acceptance of the independent bar was that the decision to join it no longer had to be clandestine. Early discussions about the opening of Hanson Chambers, for example, took place discreetly in the Stock Exchange Club; as did those three or four years later for Jeffcott. But by 1984, Brian Hayes never thought twice about voicing his interest in leaving Norman Waterhouse to join the independent bar. In fact, by then his problem was replacing himself. When he approached Tony Besanko and explained why he was leaving Norman Waterhouse, instead of finding a replacement he discovered Besanko had also been planning on joining the bar. Hayes ended up with another member for the new chambers.

Jeffcott Chambers was one of the most ambitious projects of the period. Neil Lowrie was a senior partner of Olsson Lowrie which employed around twenty lawyers. Normally partners in the larger firms like this were opposed to the independent bar, but Lowrie was an entrepreneur and the prospect of establishing chambers and a new career appealed to him. There is talk of an attempt in 1980 to set up new chambers in the burnt-out King's Music Hall on the corner of Carrington and King William Streets. That must have seemed too daunting and the project never went ahead. Lowrie set his sights on the old Supreme Court Hotel at 7 Gouger Street, which the government was planning to demolish.

Lowrie met with the Minister of Public Works, Dean Brown, who was amenable to leasing the building as long as there was no cost involved to the government. An architect estimated it would cost around $100,000 to renovate and Lowrie obtained a ten-year lease, renewable at the Court's discretion. Chief Justice Len King had been interested in the old hotel building as a potential judge's chambers. Originally, Lowrie only envisaged filling the top floor and leasing the ground floor to Butterworths, but the state government would not permit it. But during the nine months the old hotel took to restore, interest in the new chambers grew. By the time it was completed Neil Lowrie could easily fill both floors with a total of twelve chambers. Out of the twelve barristers who filled them when Jeffcott Chambers opened, three were already practising as barristers – Kelvyn Prescott, Len Lindon and John von Doussa – and the other nine were leaving firms.

Jeffcott's approach from the beginning was to present itself to the profession as a corporate identity in its own right rather than as a group of separate, unlinked individuals. The reason for this approach was to adapt to Adelaide's in-house tradition, still very strong then in the early 1980s. In day-to-day practice the way this worked was that the founding clerk of chambers, Kate Jennings, obtained briefs from the firms and then found a barrister. The firms did not have to try and find an individual at Jeffcott Chambers themselves. If the one they originally sought was not available, Kate would guarantee another barrister would take the brief. This style borrowed the best from the traditional English clerking system without going so far as to become the only method available, the trap that the eastern states fell into.

The founding members of Jeffcott Chambers, while continuing the tradition begun at Hanson earlier of naming chambers after South Australian legal personalities, also linked itself to the English tradition. The company formed by the members of chambers for the purpose of leasing and administrating Jeffcott Chambers is known as Rumpole. John Mortimer, creator of the fearlessly individualistic archetype of the English criminal bar, came to Adelaide in July 1982 to formally open the chambers and signed the wall in the library under the photograph of John Jeffcott. That piece of wall now is a feature at Jeffcott's new address on Flinders Street.

At the same time Jeffcott opened, Hanson Chambers doubled in size to house six barristers. With each expansion, the independent bar seemed also to increase its workload. The new barristers quickly became busy. The legal profession was adapting to the increasing importance of its specialist independent branch. But by 1984, despite 16% of legal practitioners being female, only one had signed the bar roll in twenty years – Pam Cleland.

Women at the independent bar

The single biggest change in the eight-century history of the common law legal profession is the entry of women in the twentieth century.

The first female lawyer in the British Empire was Clara Brett Martin, who was finally admitted as a solicitor and barrister in Canada in 1897. She had been awarded her degree in 1890 from Trinity College, Toronto, but it took her seven years of fighting the Ontario Law Society to gain the right to admission. She practised until her early death in 1923 from a heart attack and she never married.

In England, the first female solicitor was Carrie Morrison, who was admitted in 1922. The same year, Ivy Williams was the first woman called to the bar in England. She had completed her studies in 1903 and had to wait for the 1919 Act in Great Britain to "amend the law with respect to disqualifications on account of sex". After having waited so long, Ivy Williams declined Inner Temple's call and instead went to teach at Oxford. But Helena Normanton accepted, and in 1949, was one of the first two women that year appointed to silk in England.

In Australia Victoria was the first state to allow women to practise law, from 6 April 1903, followed by Tasmania in 1904, Queensland in 1905 and South Australia in 1911. The first practising female lawyer in Australia was Flos Greig in Victoria, admitted in 1905. Ada Evans was the first female law graduate in 1902, but she had to fight the New South Wales governments to gain the right to practise, and it took her almost twenty years. It was 1921 when New South Wales finally allowed women to practise. By this time, like Ivy Williams in England, Ada Evans had had enough. Although she was admitted, she refused to practise because of the lapse of time since her studies.

The University of Adelaide had always permitted women to attend classes since it started teaching in 1876, and to be awarded degrees from 1881. But the first female law student was only born around then – Doris Egerton Jones began studying some law subjects in 1909 and graduated with a BA in 1911. The year after, Mary Kitson began her law studies and in 1917, she was admitted as South Australia's first female lawyer. The second was Aileen Constance Ingleby, in 1921, daughter of Rupert Ingleby KC (Jnr) and granddaughter of Rupert Ingleby KC (Snr). Aileen Ingleby was in a University of Adelaide hockey team with Dorothy Christine Somerville, and talked her into taking up law. Somerville had already taken an honours arts degree in classics in 1918, and in 1922, she became South Australia's third female legal practitioner.

The first women experienced quite severe discrimination from their male fellow students. In 1911 a male law student wrote to *The Register* – a daily morning paper in Adelaide – complaining about the fact that if women join the classes, any discussion of "immoral considerations" in criminal and contract law would not be possible: "I think it will be unfair to make students pay heavy fees for lectures and then have important questions missed because females invade the classroom." He foresaw the subsequent and inevitable decline in legal education.

The worst recorded treatment took place in the University of Sydney in the 1920s. Even though the New South Wales government had legislated in 1921 to permit women to practise, male students taunted Marie Beuzeville Byles and Sibyl Gibbs with foot-stomping and "cat-calling". In South Australia, Mary Kitson found that in 1924 when she got married, her partners no longer wished to practise with her. She found a solution: that year she and Dorothy Somerville established Australia's first female legal practice.

Mary Kitson eventually moved to Sydney and worked in publishing and in 1950, she moved to New York to take charge of the United Nations affairs on the Status of Women. Somerville only gave up practice not long before her death in 1992, at the age of ninety-four. She was also the first woman in Australia to take on another woman as an articled clerk. This was her niece, Sesca Zelling, wife of Howard.

Kitson's and Somerville's achievements forged the path for women in South Australia, and the baton was readily taken by Roma Mitchell. She was admitted at the end of 1934. Yet despite becoming Australia's first female Queen's Counsel in 1960, it was still hard then for women to get articles. In 1963 Margaret Nyland – who would later be appointed first to the District Court, and then the Supreme Court – was beginning to lose hope. Her father was a boiler-maker, and after an accident, he had to drive taxis. One of his regular passengers was lawyer John Davey. By a stroke of luck, Davey knew Pam Cleland, who took on Nyland's articles.

From the late 1970s women began studying law in greater and greater numbers. In 1977, one sixth of the law students at the University of Adelaide were female; within eight years the proportion had reached one half. By 2004, the proportion was edging towards 60%, where it has remained. Admissions to practice for female lawyers have been at least equal or more for over a decade, but the profession overall is presently just less than two-thirds male.

South Australia's independent bar has therefore not only developed together with a massive expansion of the legal profession, but also with an exponential increase in the number of females studying law. By June 2018 in Australia, the Law Council Equitable Briefing Policy Annual Report found women made up 52% of solicitors, but just 23% of the independent State bars. In South Australia in 2020 46 of the 230 barristers on the SA Bar Association website were female: 20%. Out of the 47 silks appointed from 2006 to 2018 in South Australia, 7 were women.

Female Queen's Counsel in South Australia's independent bar – Lindy Powell, Frances Nelson, Marie Shaw and Robyn Layton – began their careers around the 1960s and 1970s and reported not being aware of discrimination. Two of them, Lindy Powell and Robyn Layton, attribute their opportunities to getting advocacy experience in their early career to the strong support of a male employer, the late Elliott Johnston.

There has been a general trend since the 1970s to attribute the small percentages of females in any profession – not just the legal one – to continuing internal discrimination from established males. Former High Court judge Mary Gaudron showed ample evidence to support this in her talk to the Women Lawyers Association of New South Wales in June 2002.[1] The most glaring statistic she drew attention to was the fact that out of the 308 senior counsel at the New South Wales Bar, only seven were female. The Australian total for senior counsel was around 30 females out of a total of 700.

One factor why we will not yet, if ever, see a legal profession and judiciary (which mainly comes from the independent bar) that reflects the percentage of female admissions to practice is potentially family. As a senior woman said: "I hate to say it because I'm a rabid feminist, but we women find it much more difficult to make the choice to turn our backs on families."[2]

An article in *The Weekend Australian* in 2003 drew attention to the fact that the daughter of High Court Chief Justice Murray Gleeson had to quit practice as a barrister after eight years "because of difficulties balancing work and family."[3] Gleeson asked the New South Wales Bar Association about the establishment of a creche:

> I was told it was difficult and expensive to do that because of the need to comply with regulatory requirements.[4]

Statistics quoted in this same article show what happens with women's careers at the New South Wales bar, of which women made up 14.9%:

> A 2002 survey found 108 women who had practised for up to four years, but the figure almost halved to 57 women in the five-to-nine year category. By contrast, men's numbers increased from 303 to 355.

Even if the number of new barristers joining each year was precisely balanced between male and female, the overall percentage of males would always be higher if males stay longer. In South Australia until 2003 there have been 34 women sign the bar roll. In the following ten years, until 2013, a further 35 signed the roll. Of those 35, 20 were in chambers as of 2020, 6 were judicial officers and 9 had left the independent bar.

Another factor occasionally mentioned is that the common law is an adversarial system, and traditionally appeared to favour a masculine voice and a ruthless attitude to one's opponent. In contrast, the French legal profession is neither an adversarial system nor has a separate bar. In 2018, out of a total of 65,480 lawyers in France, 36,303 were women – 55%.

However, one of South Australia's successful female barristers, Melissa Perry, has challenged the value of aggression:

> (...) aggression is very rarely, if ever, in the client's best interests. Barristers are engaged in the task of persuasion, and judges, as intelligent and diligent decision-makers, want thorough preparation, strong analytical abilities, a deep understanding of legal principle and sound judgment on the part of the advocates who appear before them. It is the application of these skills which are the more useful to us. These are the tools of persuasion and I can assure you that they are not unequally endowed upon any particular gender.[4a]

Justice Perry stressed the value of support and encouragement from senior barristers to juniors, but also of personal resilience.

The factors that explain the enduring small percentage of women barristers are no doubt complex, but the increasing judicial appointments point to a improving future, if exasperatingly slow. It may also be that mediation may continue to grow as an alternative to the adversarial trial and new models such as this do not bring the baggage of legacy practices.

Since 2014 the South Australian Bar Association has had a permanent Women at the Bar sub-committee, of which the first chair was Sashi Maharaj. The committee aims for "equity at the bar", that is to encourage women to join the independent bar, support the retention of women and to optimise opportunities for women to advance their careers as a barrister or in the law generally. The committee also participates with the Australian Bar Association, the Law Society of South Australia and the Law Council of Australia in implementing gender equity policies and strategies.

The Labor and Liberal South Australian governments have increased the appointments of women to judical roles. Of the 23 District Court judges and masters, 9 are female (40%) and of the 15 Supreme Court judges and masters, 4 are female (26%).

The Labor Government's 1990 challenge to the value of the independent bar in South Australia

By 1980 the South Australian legal profession numbered around 1000 practitioners, and the independent bar numbered less than twenty. In the next ten years the total profession in private practice grew to 1500 and the independent bar quintupled to 100. Around 500 more lawyers worked for the government. The Dunstan decade had produced masses of new legislation and both civil and criminal trials were growing increasingly complex. The growth of the bar was certainly possible due to this general increase in the demand for legal services. The pool of specialists whose skills in court and in advising on matters that might reach court had become a crucial component of South Australia's legal profession. The independent bar grew in spontaneous response to the evolving needs of the profession. It grew and thrived because it met these needs.

This is what distinguishes South Australia's independent bar from those in New South Wales and its two daughter-states, Queensland and Victoria. These bars are better described as separate than independent, as they were established in an artificial attempt to imitate the divided legal profession in England. This artificial division was directly the result of the persistent and stubborn efforts of English trained barristers William Charles Wentworth (1790–1872) and Robert Wardell (1794–1834).

Wentworth (already known for crossing the Blue Mountains in 1813 with Blaxland and Lawson) met Wardell in Cambridge in the 1820s and the two were admitted to the Sydney legal profession in 1824, demanding division from the first day.[5] Chief Justice Sir Francis Forbes (1784-1841) did not believe the nascent colony of 70,000 (including 20,000 convicts) could support it, and it was ten years before the two mavericks won, when the Chief Justice was outnumbered by two judges more sympathetic to the cause, Dowling and Burton.

The circumstances in which the division of the profession became law provoked bitter challenges that lasted a further thirteen years, and included a contempt of court charge against the anti-division newspaper *The Australian* (not related to the one of the same title founded in 1964 by Murdoch), founded around 1824 by Wentworth and Wardell, but later sold.

Wentworth's and Wardell's incentive for division of the Australian profession had nothing to do with an interest in local justice being better served. They were ambitious for political power, and they intended to use law and newspaper proprietorship to obtain it. They were also influenced by the fact that when they left England in 1824 solicitors were still not seen as professional lawyers – they were probably viewed like paralegals are today. When Wentworth and Wardell arrived in Sydney, as members of an Inn of Court, they were offended by the idea of sharing legal practice with attorneys and solicitors, who they saw as non-professionals. The status of solicitors was only professionalised in 1834 with the founding of the Law Society.

That was coincidentally the year that division was formalised in Sydney. Wardell was murdered a few months short of seeing it, but Wentworth went on to dominate New South Wales politics. His thirst for power, even once established in politics, was never satiated and in the 1850s he even suggested to much laughter that the New South Wales upper house be made hereditary.[6]

From their origins in the ambitions of Wentworth and Wardell, the three separate bars of the populous eastern states developed as more or less faithful models of England's, as opposed to the independent bars that developed in the 1960s and 1970s in the territories and smaller states in direct response to needs. By the 1970s and 1980s, better-educated populations began expecting access to justice. The problem was its cost. Some traditional practices at the English and eastern Australian bars stood out as not only anachronistic, but as artificially inflating the fees lawyers could charge.

The result were a series of government studies recommending reforms not just to archaic laws but to the structure of the legal profession itself. New South Wales produced a series of studies during the 1980s, and Western Australia produced an inquiry in 1983. In 1989 in the United Kingdom, the Lord Chancellor published "The Work and Organisation of the Legal Profession", which was known as the Green Paper. The South Australian Attorney-General, the Hon. Chris Sumner MLC released his own "Green Paper" in October 1990. This was a few months after the Law Reform Commission of Victoria released its paper on the cost of litigation in May. Sumner aimed to reduce the costs of legal services and he blamed in part the independent bar. The Green Paper and some of the responses provide us with the opportunity to discuss the relevance of South Australia's independent bar in relation to specific points which it brought up.

The "Green" Paper - early 1990s

Litigation has always been out of the reach of the average citizen. In a study of 208 English barristers who became judges between 1727 and 1875, twenty of them had earned more than 10,000 pounds and three or four of them more than 20,000 pounds.[7] In 1928, Lord Maugham earned 25,000 and Lord Birkett 30,000 pounds. The average income then was around 100 pounds a year. According to the Australian Bureau of Statistics in Australia, for the financial year 1998–1999 the nation's 3704 barristers grossed average fees each of $227,537. Their average net income after costs was $146,000.

These figures vary enormously between individuals, and so must be interpreted with care. In England in 1928, despite the huge incomes of Lord Maugham and Lord Birkett, the median English barrister's income was estimated at just 600 pounds – fifty times less than Birketts, but still six times the average income of that time.[8] In Australia, barristers annual incomes are a private matter, but Sydney barrister Stephen Archer, who had a long-running public dispute with the Tax Office, was reported to have earned $1.4 million in 1989.[9] The Tax Office was demanding payment of $5.7million for eleven years, which suggests they believed his annual income over that time was around one million dollars per year. These figures give an example, if isolated, of the potential income of a senior barrister in New South Wales nearer the end of the twentieth century.

Regardless of how much barristers' incomes vary between individuals, it is clear that in general those at the bar earn well over the average income. Therefore, their fees will certainly be prohibitive for the average client. Chris

Sumner believed that if justice was too costly, then there was no equality before the law:

> Does that equality exist when the legal rights of citizens can only be realised by the rich and powerful? The public perception is that some citizens are more equal than others before the courts because they can afford the high cost of legal representation whereas others can't.[10]

There is no dispute that legal services are very expensive and that a government should do what it can to make them more accessible. But Chris Sumner believed however that "the situation had worsened in recent years",[11] and in his Green Paper it is clear that he placed the blame on the emerging independent bar. He did not provide any solid evidence to back up this perception.

The Green Paper made a number of proposals, some of which the government wanted to implement as soon as possible. The first was to repeal Section 6 of the Legal Practitioners Act 1981 which allowed the judges of the Supreme Court at any time to divide the legal profession into barristers and solicitors, and in its place affirm the maintenance of a fused profession. The government must have feared that the South Australian independent bar might eventually gather enough power to force division, particularly when a future Supreme Court bench was mainly made up of former members of the independent bar.

The second proposal aimed to reverse Chief Justice Len King's 1979 direction that new appointees to Queen's Counsel in firms would be required to leave and practise independently. Chris Sumner believed that the present system of appointing Queen's Counsel led directly to the artificial inflation of barristers' fees. His solution was to expand its base dramatically to include solicitors, government lawyers and academics. The aim was to dilute the title so it would no longer be the senior rank for barristers, and therefore, end the higher tier of charges.

A third proposal recommended changes to the Professional Conduct Rules to allow clients direct access to a barrister, including a Queen's Counsel. The implication was obviously that the solicitor's intermediate role between client and barrister may add an unnecessary expense to the client's costs.

Other proposals in the Green Paper recommended the increased use of paralegals and more detailed estimates to be given to clients on their likely legal costs. There were also invitations for comment on the possible abolition of barristers' immunity from civil liability and the possibility of allowing solicitors and accountants to practise within the same partnerships. There was also a proposal for the abandonment of wigs, bar jackets and jabots in the higher courts.

The South Australian Bar Association (SABA) responded in detail, pointing out a number of fundamental flaws. One was that the authors of the Green Paper did not consult with the judiciary, the Law Society or the Bar Association. As a result, many of their ideas and the efforts in articulating them had been wasted as they were incorrectly founded. Another basic flaw was despite the "laudable objects" of the Green Paper to obtain cost effective legal services, most of the proposals in it would not have any such consequences:

> These proposals are largely related to matters such as eligibility for appointment of Queen's Counsel, legislative entrenchment of the fusion of the profession, so-called restrictive trade practices of the Bar and changes to court attire. The adoption of all or any of the suggested proposals would not broaden community access to justice. Nor would their adoption increase the efficiency with which legal services are delivered or reduce their cost.[12]

The Bar Association also disputed the term "separate bar":

> There is no "separate" bar in South Australia. All legal practitioners are admitted to the same bar [...] Those who wish to specialise in the field of advocacy may voluntarily sign the Roll of Counsel and thereby signify publicly an intention to practise solely as counsel. Those who do so are in no sense "separate" from the wider legal profession. They are "independent" of any particular solicitor or firm of solicitors and, if description be necessary, they should be described as members of the "independent" bar.[13]

It is of course this independence from firms that allowed the very growth of the independent bar. Solicitors could refer clients to an independent barrister and know that they would not be poached. The benefit to the client since the establishment of the independent bar is that they can choose the best qualified barrister to deal with their litigation while maintaining the important ongoing relationship necessary with their solicitor for their day-to-day legal needs.

The Bar Association was also alarmed at the implied antipathy towards the development of the independent bar:

> [T]he bias against the independent bar does not appear to be based on a knowledge or understanding of current practice in this state. For example, it is recommended that a number of so-called "restrictive practices" of the independent bar be discouraged. However, the practices identified have never been adopted here. These recommendations suggest the authors of the Green Paper have never practised in South Australia. If this is correct, the lack of prior consultation referred to above is all the more lamentable.[14]

Chief Justice Len King had been Labor Attorney-General in the Dunstan government for five years before being appointed to the Supreme Court. He was an early proponent of the independent bar, and had introduced the undertaking in 1979 for Queen's Counsel to join the bar. King was also a proponent of a more efficient justice system, and since his appointment as Chief Justice in 1978, he had pushed for numerous reforms to speed up listings and length of trials. In this, his goal was the same as Sumner's, and to Len King the independent bar was a crucial contributor:

> There is contemporary emphasis upon efficient administration of the business of the courts whereby the resources provided to the courts are used to maximum effectiveness with a view to containing costs and minimising delay. That requires that hearings occur on the date fixed and that adjournments be not granted on the ground that the counsel originally briefed is unavailable because of a conflict of engagements. For such a system to operate without injustice it is essential that there be a pool of competent counsel available to accept late briefs and to handle them capably. That pool is the separate bar. If there were no separate bar or an inadequate separate bar, the courts would be faced with the necessity of adjourning cases to avoid injustice. There would be much wastage of judicial resources with consequent delays and additional cost. That occurred in this State before the existence of a separate bar and is the bane of judicial administration in jurisdictions where there is no separate bar. An adequate separate bar is an indispensable requisite, under present conditions, of an efficient court system.[15]

King drew attention to the fact that the members of the independent bar were markedly more skilled as a result of their specialisation:

> The resultant improvement in the standard of advocacy greatly assists the court in reaching a just decision and reduces the time occupied in the presentation of cases. Both the quality and the efficiency of the delivery of justice is thereby enhanced.

He believed that the independent bar reduced rather than increased the cost of litigation:

> Any weakening of the separate bar would therefore be seriously detrimental to the interests of the community both directly by affecting the cost and quality of legal services available and indirectly by undermining the efficiency and quality of the judicial system.

The Chief Justice was very alarmed to read in the Green Paper of the proposal to revert to the previous system of Queen's Counsel being able to practise from within firms. The attention in the Green Paper given to changes proposed to Queen's Counsel are really at the heart of its whole intent. If the top tier of barristers could be devalued, then fees would fall all the way down the line. King noted that the writers of the Green Paper had no understanding of the previous vague requirements of Queen's Counsel, nor of the way firms acquired them to gain a competitive advantage:

> I summarise my position by stating that the proposals in the discussion paper as to the appointment of Queen's Counsel are retrograde and deplorable. Theories may be spun in other jurisdictions, but in this State we have had practical experience of Queen's Counsel practising in firms and the detrimental consequences of such practice. (...) there is no excuse in this State for reverting to a system which has been experienced and discredited.

Justice John Perry also wrote to the Attorney-General. Perry was one of the first Queen's Counsel appointed after Len King's 1979 requirement and his comparison of his experience as a counsel in a firm with being independent is the perfect illustration of what the South Australian independent bar stands for. When he was with Kelly & Co. he acted regularly for the Australian Hotels Association:

> I had a substantial practice in the Licensing Court, but because of the affiliations of my firm, it was inconceivable that I could represent interests other than hotel interests.[16]

As far as he could recall, he was never offered briefs for opposing interests:

> All of that changed when I went to the separate Bar. I then received and accepted briefs to appear on behalf of applicants for retail liquor store licences in particular, which, generally speaking, were the most hotly contested applications dealt with in that jurisdiction and which were argued against strong opposition from hotel interests. During my time at the separate Bar I also acted for hotel interests,

> particularly on appeal to the Full Court of the Supreme Court. I think it would be fair to say that my practice at the Bar was more or less evenly divided between hotel interests, and clients opposed to those interests.

Justice Perry also experienced a similar situation regarding his industrial practice. While at Kelly & Co. he regularly represented the Chamber of Commerce and Industry and the Employer's Federation. He never was offered briefs to represent union or employee interests:

> The reverse was true once I was at the separate Bar. I then regularly received briefs in the industrial area from both employer interests and unions. Indeed, I considered it most important if I was properly to discharge my role as Queen's Counsel, that I exhibit in my professional life no predilection for or affiliation with any political or other sectional interests, and that I make myself available to anyone who wished to brief me.

Solicitor-General John Doyle, who succeeded King as Chief Justice in 1995, echoed concerns about the impact of allowing Queen's Counsel to practise from firms. He believed that, as in the past, it would reduce accessibility, as Queen's Counsel in firms would be reluctant to accept briefs "for interests which conflict with those of the firm's major clients".[17]

Submissions from the Legal Services Commission echoed the concerns of Len King, John Perry and John Doyle. The Legal Services Commission was acutely sensitive to barristers' fees as in the previous year it had paid out almost seven and a half million dollars to private practitioners on behalf of its clients. On the issue of removing court attire, all these correspondents were unanimous in retaining it. The example that stood out was the experience of the Family Court:

> When that Court was established in 1975, formal attire was prohibited. After more than ten years experience of informality, the Court adopted traditional legal attire for the purpose (inter alia) of restoring formality and giving public expression to the important principle that Judge and counsel are performing functions in the legal process.[18]

The authors of the Green Paper had not consulted the reasons behind the Federal Labor Government making that change.

Perhaps it is not surprising that the independent bar was defended by its association and those who signed its Roll. On the opposite side of the argument were letters from firms such as Thomson Simmons & Co., Kelly & Co. and Finlaysons, all supporting the Green Paper's proposal that silks should be able once again to practise from firms. But the Law Society, which is the official regulator of the entire legal profession in South Australia, strongly defended the independent bar and the requirement that Queen's Counsel must be independent:

> To allow Queen's Counsel when appointed to remain in partnership is a retrograde step. The development of the independent bar in South Australia is testament to the willingness of persons to practice independent of partnership but in co-operation with other barristers in order to provide the most cost effective service to consumers. Those barristers thereby expose themselves to competition in the development of their skills and knowledge and also give the greatest possible choice of barrister to a person in the legal profession who may wish to brief counsel in any matter.[19]

The competitive nature of practice at the independent bar insures that fees are not being artificially inflated. Unlike in the eastern states, in South Australia there is competition with amalgam firms who conduct much of their own counsel work, for example Craig Caldicott. If the independent bar grew unjustifiably expensive, it would price itself out of existence and eventually disappear. The opposite has in fact happened – it has grown in size quickly and exponentially.

In September 1991 Chris Sumner presented a paper at the Australian Legal Convention in Adelaide, and reiterated his concern about the cost of legal services. He had not been convinced at all by the arguments from those defending the independent bar. He continued to place the blame firmly on the office of Queen's Counsel:

> In 1979 the Chief Justice required all those recommended for silk to undertake to practice at the separate bar. In my view this was a retrograde step. It tends to encourage an undesirable division of the profession. Those who wish to take silk tend to go to the separate bar rather than remain in firms. The firms then lose their advocacy skills and the undesirable features of a divided profession emerge even though the profession, in law, is a fused one.

Retrograde is moving backwards. To once again allow Queen's Counsel to remain in firms would be a retrograde step, which is why Len King and the Law Society used the term in their responses to the Green Paper. It is not clear why Chris Summer thought that the requirement to practise at the "separate" bar was retrograde, since that requirement never existed previously in South Australia. The Attorney-General went further:

> The competitive market for legal services is distorted by the creation of Q.C.'s as presently appointed and they encourage a divided profession.

Chief Justice Len King intended his 1979 requirement on new silk appointments both to attract more lawyers to the independent bar and to strengthen its nascent reputation. He never intended to set the South Australian legal profession on the path to eventual division in the image of the eastern States or the English bar. He did believe that specialisation in advocacy would lead to an increase in skills and a corresponding increase in efficiency in matters before the courts. Just as a point of comparison, the medical profession is not considered to be hoping for a division between general practitioners and specialists because of the existence of, for example, the Royal Australasian College of Surgeons.

Many aspects of the Green Paper showed a serious misunderstanding of the independent bar, and a paranoia of its potential development. Nevertheless, Len King would have agreed with Chris Sumner in its central tenet, and that was litigation was out of range of the ordinary member of the community. At that same conference the then Chief Justice acknowledged:

> The harsh reality is that there is abroad in the community a pervasive sense of dissatisfaction with the legal system and, to an extent, with the legal profession which is part of it. This sense of dissatisfaction exists in all sections of the community and extends from the board rooms of large corporations to the person on the street.
> (...)
> If you ask the ordinary citizen what he thinks of the legal system, he will tell you that it is irrelevant to him. He will tell you that he could not consider embarking on litigation to assert or protect his rights. [20]

King went even further to suggest that the basic purpose of a system of justice, "namely that it makes justice available to all, is not being achieved, even approximately". He warned his audience that the legal profession had to devise and implement the changes necessary to enable the system to achieve its purpose, or it may "face unwelcome and probably ill-advised external intervention". Four years later Len King again expressed his regret that the greatest imperfection of the legal system is restriction on access to the courts because of the cost of litigation.[21]

The anomaly in Attorney-General Chris Sumner's fight against the cost of litigation in South Australia was that during the Green Paper debate he introduced a new daily trial fee. At the 1991 Australian Legal Convention President of the Law Council of Australia, David Miles, criticised the South Australian Attorney-General:

> It is hypocritical of the Government to blame the cost of justice on the legal profession and then to introduce high fees simply for approaching a court seeking to take legal action or proceeding with a legal hearing.
>
> I am particularly disappointed with the approach taken by the South Australian Attorney-General. He has taken the opportunity provided to him at this Convention to criticise costs in the profession, yet he has recently imposed a new fee of $150 per day just for hearing a case. Mr Sumner is effectively making South Australians rent their own courtrooms.[22]

That fee was roughly 30% higher than the average daily earnings for 1991 of $110. Rather than setting the example in reducing the cost of litigation, the Labor Government of the day added to it. During the years since, these trial fees have risen much higher than salaries. These government imposed daily fees had risen to $1007 in 2004 for the Supreme Court and $2,702.00 in 2020.

The primary legacy of the Green Paper debate has been to change Section 6 of the Legal Practitioners Act 1981 so that the Supreme Court judges no longer have the option to divide the profession. Subsection (1) now reads:

> It is Parliament's intention that the legal profession should continue to be a fused profession of barristers and solicitors.

The Section allows for South Australian practitioners to specialise either as solicitors or barristers, and to be members of a group of similar practitioners. The South Australian Bar Association is not seen as inconsistent with Parliament's intention, but neither is it obligatory for a barrister to be a member of it. Queen's Counsel are specially allowed for in Subsection 3a, and are expected to practise according to the office.

The fused nature of the legal profession in South Australia, as in the other "fused" States and territories, is its strength. The formally divided professions have been guilty of inflexible and anti-competitive practices, and if that was what Chris Sumner feared, he was correct. Even in Victoria, which has officially had a fused profession since 1891, division operates with little distinction from that in New South Wales and Queensland. One of the most negative aspects of the separate bar in Victoria is the Victorian Bar Council's monopoly of ownership of the sets of chambers in the Melbourne courts precinct. Being an independent barrister in that State is legally possible, but practically difficult for those individuals who do not wish to join the vast ant colonies of Owen Dixon Chambers, Douglas Menzies Chambers and so on. If Chris Sumner has prevented South Australia from any risk of a future bar resembling those of the eastern States and London in any way, then his contribution to the profession was a positive one.

Because the South Australian independent bar is not propped up by artificial, antiquated legal structures, its survival and prosperity has always been entirely due to its relevance and competitiveness. In the three decades since the Green Paper, the independent bar has continued to grow and flourish – from 100 barristers then there are around 230. In 1990 there were eleven sets of chambers; by 2020 there were at least double that. These small sets of chambers – plus many barristers who practise alone – are what gives the South Australian independent bar its independence. It also permits growth and evolution to happen quickly in response to needs. If there is an opening for two or three extra barristers, they can set up themselves.

The Bar Readers Course

The introduction in August 2002 of the Bar Readers' Course was an important development in the continuing evolution of the South Australian independent bar. Across the older and larger eastern bars, courses had been operating for some time. Dean Clayton was the driving force behind the establishment of the Course and Nigel Wilson prepared the inaugural curriculum to satisfy the requirements of the existing readers models in Queensland, New South Wales and Victoria.

After slight trepidation from some established barristers that they would be asked to train their future competitors for no pay, the course soon proved a success and in 2008 made compulsory for all new signatories to the Bar Roll, around the same time the chair of its local organising committee was made a permanent member of the Australian Bar Council.

The first course in 2002 began with six readers and since then there have been around 10 per year. The course only missed 2003 when there were too few applicants and 2020 due to the coronvirus. By 2014 around 85 people had completed the Bar Readers' Course and by February 2020, that number would have easily passed 100.

The 2002 course was 83 contact hours over a 10-week period, by 2013 the contact hours were able to be reduced to around 50. Only barristers and judges do the training, still for no payment, and there has not been a plan to outsource training.

Since 2008, again with the exception of the coronavirus in 2020, a Residential Trial Advocacy Course has been held alternately in Adelaide and Perth. In 2012 Chris Bleby became the first reader to take silk, and in 2020 he was appointed to the Supreme Court's Court of Appeal.

Endnotes

1 Speech for Women Lawyers Association of New South Wales, 50th Anniversary Gala Dinner. Link to http://www.hcourt.gov.au/speeches/gaudronj/gaudronj_wlansw.html.

2 "Why the bar is too high for female lawyers". *The Advertiser,* Saturday, August 30, 2003, p 19.

3 "Creche for the bar, urges Gleeson". *The Weekend Australian*, August 30-31, 2003, p 8.

4 As above.

4a The Hon Justice Melissa Perry, 5 April 2014. "Women at the Bar: aspirations and inspirations." Womens Barristers Forum, NSW Bar Association Common Room. Available at https://www.fedcourt.gov.au/digital-law-library/judges-speeches/justice-perry/perry-j-20140405.

5 For a good general account of the events leading to the division of the New South Wales legal profession, see J R S Forbes, *The Divided Legal Profession in Australia,* Sydney: Law Book Company, 1979, pp. 31-47.

6 Forbes, p. 35.

7 Richard L. Abel. *The Legal Profession in England and Wales*. Oxford: Blackwell, 1988, p 122.

8 Same.

9 Ellen Connolly, *Sydney Morning Herald*, 20 February 2003, http://www.smh.com.au/articles/2003/02/19/1045638361018.html

10 Speech given by the Hon. Chris Sumner MLC, Attorney-General at the Australian Legal Convention, 9 September 1991.

11 As above.

12 Submission of the South Australian Bar Association Inc. on the Green Paper on the Legal Profession, February 1991, p 2.

13 Same, p 3.

14 Same.

15 Letter from the Chief Justice to the Attorney-General, dated 19 November 1990.

16 Letter from Justice John Perry to the Attorney-General, dated 13 February 1991.

17 Letter from the Solicitor-General to the Attorney-General, dated 6 March 1991.

18 Submission of the South Australian Bar Association, as above, p 14.

19 Law Society of South Australia's Response to the Attorney-General's Green Paper on the Legal Profession, p. 10.

20 Speech given by the Hon. the Chief Justice, Len King, at the Australian Legal Convention, 12 September 1991.

21 Address of Chief Justice Len King for the special sitting of the Supreme Court to mark his retirement, 28 April 1995.

22 "New tax increases cost of justice". *Australian Law News*, October 1991, p. 39

Part Two

Bluestone

Chapter Three

Adelaide Chambers
The Bluestone Phenomenon

Howard Zelling and Christopher Legoe's initial choice of a relatively small historical building for Adelaide's first set of barristers chambers established a tradition that continues to define South Australia's independent bar.

There are twenty-five sets of chambers listed on the South Australian Bar Association website and ten of these are or were housed in small historical buildings. But regardless of the historical status of the building, the single characteristic that defines the South Australian independent bar from all others in Australia is they have continued to form in small groups. The largest are Jeffcott, Edmund Barton and Murray, with accommodation for either side of twenty barristers. In contrast, the other bars in Australia have concentrated their members into relatively few sets of chambers, some numbering in the several hundreds like Owen Dixon Chambers in Melbourne. Even Perth's independent bar – a twin in terms of size and age – still has around half of its bar located in Francis Burt Chambers.

Despite forming in small groups, Adelaide sets of chambers have nevertheless enjoyed longevity, a sign of the strength of the reputation that their members have built up. The first three that opened in the city – Bar, Hanson and Jeffcott – remain open and have thrived. Two of those that have closed are earlier groupings of more or less the same barristers: Wellington Chambers relocated from North Adelaide to Market Street, City, and became Market Street Chambers in 1986; moving again in 1991 to become Mitchell Chambers.

Many barristers tend to stay in one set of chambers during the course of their career. Several have been in a single set of chambers their whole career. Often new members of a set of chambers are given the smallest room as its previous occupant moves into a bigger one becoming available after a retirement or an appointment to the bench of a senior member. If in the meantime, if a bigger room is available at another set of chambers, the member may move.

Sometimes barristers prefer a much smaller group. David Greenwell was one of the founders of Edmund Barton Chambers. As it grew he discovered that he preferred the relative autonomy of his own independent chambers. He set up Victoria Chambers in 1996 and remained the sole member until Roger Sallis joined him in 2000. Others prefer a sole practice. Barristers who set up practice in the suburbs of Adelaide have often found that this can prove inconvenient during trials. Sets of chambers outside the CBD have generally been of short duration with the exception of Libra. The most immediate issue is all-day casual parking near the appropriate court. This problem disappears if one is already based in the courts precinct. The other reason for the relatively short existence of suburban chambers is that they have often been founded at or next to the home of a barrister. When that barrister decides to retire, move or sell, the set of chambers is disbanded. This is different from the sets founded in the city, which are more usually formed as distinct entities from their founders.

In some instances barristers have changed chambers for purely personal reasons. The independent bar attracts independent people with strong characters. A barrister is her or his own boss. A set of chambers is not in any way comparable to a firm. Twelve barristers operating from the same premises are twelve separate sole traders who share pooled resources. But their work is their own and they are free to take it elsewhere if a problem arises that cannot be resolved.

This point raises the question of what function a set of chambers performs. Is it nothing more than shared offices, a photocopier and someone to answer the phone? Are there additional advantages to sharing the same address with people who are occasionally one's competitors for business, and opponents in court? Can a set of chambers develop its own character? In 2019 originally appointed Senior Counsels had the choice of retaining the title or changing to Queen's Counsel. If they belonged to one of the older sets of chambers were they more likely to change to the older title?

The advantages of belonging to a set of chambers as opposed to practising alone are no doubt weighed up by individual barristers at various times during their careers. There is the obvious collegial advantage of being able to wander down a corridor or up some stairs to ask advice on a problem. A barrister at the start of their career may pick up work from a senior colleague in the same chambers. At the end of a day an informal gathering around the mealroom table could help let off steam. There is also the fact that the older a set of chambers becomes, the more its name becomes engrained in the consciousness of the wider profession, and this may help attract new briefs. One thing is obvious, the majority of the independent bar in South Australia, like anywhere else in common law jurisdictions, prefer the security and collegiality of practising from a permanent set of chambers, at least for part of their careers. There are the outstanding counter-examples, Frances Nelson and Michael Abbott. Both have preferred sole chambers or small ones.

The individual listing for each set of chambers varies according to the information available on their establishment and on the length of time they have been in existence. Of the twenty-three listed, around fourteen were established in the 1980s and 1990s. The number of new sets of chambers being established since has diminished since 2000. Torrens Chambers and John Bray Chambers are in danger of disappearing with the departure of many of their members. Wright Chambers was closing at the time of publication. However, a new set set was opening at the end of 2020, Nexus, with a vision for a flexible and adaptable model to changing times and individual career paths.

The focus is on sets of chambers which in principle at least were set up as permanent and not dependent on the presence or ownership of any particular individual member. Thus the primary goal is to provide at least some record of the independent bar's evolution to those who may be curious in future decades. But this rule is not rigorously adhered to. For example, Pam Cleland's chambers is listed, because it was in existence of over twenty-five years, and Market and Wellington Chambers are listed as they are the direct ancestors of Mitchell Chambers.

Where barristers have left chambers for magisterial or judicial appointments, this is indicated, but only for the immediate appointment, not any subsequent ones.

Chambers

in order opened

Legend

MCSA Magistrates Court of South Australia
DCSA Disrict Court of South Australia
SCSA Supreme Court of South Australia
COA Court of Appeal Supreme Court SA
SCNT Supreme Court of Northern Territory
FMC Federal Magistrates Court
FC Federal Court
UA University of Adelaide
Assoc Associate member of chambers
LSSA Law Society of South Australia

Photographs courtesy of the set of chambers are attributed by letters. For example, "BC" is Bar Chambers, "DC" is Divett Chambers, etc.

Bar Chambers

34 Carrington Street, Adelaide
Opened: March, 1965

Members in approximate order of joining:

Christopher Legoe	(1965–1978) SCSA
Robin Millhouse	(1965–1982) SCSA
Michael Detmold	(1965–1968) UA
Alexander (Keith) Sangster	(1965–1970) SCSA
Robert Mohr	(1966–1970) DCSA; SCSA
Michael Birchall	(1967–1977; 1979–2015) Assoc
Brendan Burns	(1970–1972) MCSA
Francis Boylan	(1971–1972) MCSA
Anthony Russell	(1971–1980) MCSA; DCSA
Michael Noblet	(1971–1973) MCSA
Andrew Hodge	(1971–1975)
Michael David	(1973–1994) DCSA
David Angel	(1975–1989) SCNT
Christopher Cocks	(1975)
Andrew Martin	(1975–2003)
Sydney Tilmouth	(1975–1977)
Geoffrey Noble	(1976–1979)
Nicholas Birchall	(1975–1979) DCSA

Robert Cameron	(1976–
David Bright	(1976–1988) DCSA
Phillip Rice	(1976–1983) DCSA ; SCNT
(Horton) Tim Williams	(1977–1995) SCSA
Brendan Burley	(1977–1987) SCSA Master
John von Doussa	(1978–1981) SCSA; FC
John Perry	(1980–1988) SCSA
Kevin Duggan	(1980–1989) SCSA
Thomas Gray	(1982–2000) SCSA; assoc
Martin Hoile	(1982–2010)
Bruce Debelle	(1983–1990) SCSA; assoc
Stephen Apps	(1987– 2008)
Dean Clayton	(1988–2003) DCSA
(James) David Edwardson	(1988–
Simon Lane	(1989–2003)
Catherine Branson	(1989–1994) FC (Sydney)
John Sulan	(1990–1997) DCSA; SCSA; assoc
Belinda Powell	(1991–
Melissa Perry	(1992– 2006) FC (Sydney)
Michael Evans	(1994–2004) DCSA (Chief)
Ian Robertson	(1994–2006)
Malcolm Blue	(1996–2011) SCSA
Nigel Wilson	(1997–2010)
Joana Fuller	(1998–2019) DCSA

Kevin Nicholson	(1997–2003) DCSA; SCSA
Michael Abbott	(2000–2007)
Michael Burnett	(2003–2020) DCSA
Mark Hoffmann	(2003–
Mark Livesey	(2003–2020) SCSA COA
Steven Millsteed	(2003–2004) DCSA
Haroon Hassan	(2003–2005)
Charles (Sam) Abbott	(2004–
Joshua Baden Teague	(2005–2018); assoc
Adam Baker	(2006–
Brendon Roberts	(2008–
Thomas Duggan	(2011–
Kris Handshin	(2014–
Enzo Belperio	(2015–
Suzanne Mackenzie	(2018–
Damian O'Leary	(2018–
Ian Thomas	(2016–
Andrew Baillie	(2020–
Lloyd Wicks	(2020–
Helen Luu	(2020–

Bar Chambers was built in 1866 as a residence for Mr William Tomsey Cooper (1826–1904). Mr Cooper had arrived in South Australia in 1853, and worked for seven years at Government House for the Governor's Private Secretary. In 1860, he went to work for the Waterworks Department, initially as Assistant Accountant, then as Valuator. By the time he retired in 1902, it was estimated that he was responsible for around 65,000 property valuations.

According to the Sands & Macdougall directories which started appearing in the 1870s, William Cooper lived in his house in Carrington Street until the 1880s. He then leased it to a physician, Dr Frederick William Niesche, who lived upstairs and converted the ground floor into consulting rooms. The use of the house for a medical practice lasted no more than ten years. By 1896, Dr Niesche was practising from an address on Franklin Street.

From around the mid 1890s the houses were numbered, and the address became – as far as can be ascertained without searching through Lands department records – 20 Carrington Street. This was certainly the house on the eastern corner of Nelson Street. The lessee in 1896 was William Brüggemann, saddler.

Five years later – in 1901 – Mr Cooper's house was leased by Mrs Christine Eicke, and was now officially listed as a boarding house. It would remain listed as a boarding house until Christopher Legoe and Howard Zelling bought it. At that time the tenant was a Miss E G Bartsch. She had lived there since 1924, which means that it will only be in October 2005 that Bar Chambers will have occupied 34 Carrington Street longer than Miss Bartsch. There have been rumours that the boarding house provided beds for purposes that extended beyond mere accommodation, but nothing by way of a reliable eye-witness account or documentary evidence exists to support these.

In January 1965, 34 Carrington Street was sold for 10,500 pounds. Christopher Legoe contributed one half, and Howard and Sesca Zelling jointly the other half. The building then had to be refurbished to make it suitable for use as a set of chambers. R W Emery Pty Ltd was appointed builders and gradually during 1965 and 1966, Bar Chambers was remodelled.

One of the original inhabitants was A K Sangster QC, who had been working more and more independently from his firm, Mouldens. When he found out he said immediately: "I'll join you." He knew that although he was already receiving briefs from firms other than Mouldens, he would receive even more if he cut his association with them altogether. This proved correct and when he was appointed a judge of the Supreme Court in 1970, his income dropped by two-thirds.

Sangster joined Bar Chambers at the end of September 1965 and was appointed Royal Commissioner of the Royal Commission into Liquor Licensing Laws early the following year. This was an immediate hiccup in his efforts to build up his independent barrister's practice as the Royal Commission made him unavailable for a full nine months. When he finished and handed up his report, he was actually unemployed for three months. He was not too concerned as according to his diaries he had been led to believe that he would be appointed Chief Justice when Sir Mellis Napier retired. But Premier Don Dunstan appointed Dr John Bray instead, so Keith Sangster ended up with work originally destined for Bray. The Royal Commission into Liquor Licensing, incidentally, employed 30 barristers, 13 of whom became judges: John Bray QC, Len King (QC 1967), Howard Zelling QC, Andrew Wells QC, Samuel Jacobs QC, Michael White, Robert Mohr, Rod Matheson (QC 1972), R A Blackburn, Robert Fisher QC, Donald Brebner, Robert Ward (QC 1970), Frank Boylan. Two of its youngest participants both went on to become long-serving Attorneys-General: Trevor Griffin and Chris Sumner.

Robin Millhouse became an icon of South Australian public life. In April 1968 he was appointed Attorney-General under the Steel Hall Liberal government. It was the Hall–Millhouse government that established the District Courts despite strong opposition at the time from the Labor party. During the 1970s when Don Dunstan's Labor government held office, Robin Millhouse grew disenchanted with the Liberal party and for a while was part of the Liberal Movement. Later again he joined the Democrats and was the State Parliamentary Leader when he was appointed to the Supreme Court in April 1982.

In response to the ever growing demand for the services of independent barristers, six more chambers became available with some building extensions in 1975 and 1976. By 1977, when Hanson Chambers opened, fourteen barristers were practising from Bar Chambers.

Members of Bar Chambers around 1999. (Coming down stairs, visible) Dean Clayton, Michael Birchall, Malcolm Blue, Andrew Noble, Nigel Wilson, Joana Fuller, Tom Gray, David Edwardson, Melissa Perry, Steven Apps, Martin Hoile, Rob Cameron, Ian Robertson, Lindy Powell, Simon Lane. (BC)

The bluestone building that began the choice of chambers setting still common. (BC)

(Standing) John Sulan, Dean Clayton, Melissa Perry, Michael Birchall, Michael Evans, Martin Hoile, Nigel Wilson. (Seated) Simon Lane, Ian Robertson, David Edwardson, Lindy Powell, Andrew Martin, Rob Cameron. (BC)

Members of Bar Chambers around 2000. Back row: Kevin Nicholson, Michael Evans, Lindy Powell, Melissa Perry, Michael Birchall, Andrew Martin, Nigel Wilson, Martin Hoile, Dean Clayton, Stephen Apps.
Front row: David Edwardson, Simon Lane, Joana Fuller, Robert Cameron, Ian Robertson. (BC)

Hanson Chambers

56 Carrington Street, Adelaide
Opened: 4 July 1977

Members in approximate order of joining:

Timothy Anderson	(1977–2003) SCSA
John Doyle	(1977–1985) Solicitor–General, SCSA Chief Justice
David Quick	(1977–2001)
John Mansfield	(1979–1996) FC
Derek Bollen	(1979–1982) SCSA
William (Jonathan) Noye Wells	(1979–
Richard White	(1982–2004) SCSA 2004; FC 2013
Geoffrey Eames	(1986–1987) Supreme Court, Victoria
(Robert John) Dick Whitington	(1988–
Geoffrey Hackett-Jones	(1989) Parliamentary Counsel
Timothy Stanley	(1989–2011) SCSA
Kevin Nicholson	(2003–2006) DCSA; SCSA 2012
Christopher Bleby	(2004–2014) Crown Counsel; Solicitor-General 2016; SCSA COA 2020
Michael Evans	(2004–2010) Crown Solicitor 2010, Chief Judge DCSA 2016
Julie von Doussa	(2007–2008) Maternity
Benjamin Doyle	(2008–

Stephen McDonald	(2011–
Thomas Cox	(2011–
Darren Blight	(2014–2020)
Robert Williams	(2015–
Anna Wells	(2017–

Hanson Chambers was founded by Tim Anderson, John Doyle and David Quick. They initially leased half of the present building, which was comprised of a pair of maisonettes. In 1979 Don Oswald, the land agent who occupied the other maisonette, moved out. By this time, briefs were coming in steadily and Anderson, Quick and Doyle purchased the whole building. Three additional barristers joined – Derek Bollen QC, John Mansfield and Jonathan Wells.

Sir Richard Hanson, South Australia's second Chief Justice from 1861 until his death in 1876 at 71 years old. (HC)

Until this point, the set of chambers had not had a name. A decision was made after looking through some old South Australian law reports to name them after second Chief Justice, Sir Richard Hanson (1805–1876). This set a new tradition, and most new sets of chambers since have been named after a notable legal identity, usually South Australian.

Richard Hanson had been an applicant in 1835 for position of Judge of the new colony of South Australia. He had been passed over for the simple reason that he was an attorney, not a barrister, and therefore regardless of his ability, was deemed ineligible. He went to Canada in 1838 with Lord Durham to assist in an inquiry into Canadian crown lands, and to New Zealand in 1840 where he challenged the Colonial Office's management of land. In 1846 Hanson emigrated to South Australia in any case and quickly established himself as a leader at the local bar. The total profession at that time was made up of around twenty-five lawyers. He lived in Sturt Street near Whitmore Square on town acre 555, and practised from the New Exchange Chambers in King William Street.

In 1849 he appeared in 110 cases – libel, assault, murder, robbery, recovery, perjury, to name some – and in a single day was known to appear in up to four cases. In 1851 he entered politics and became Advocate-General. In 1857 when South Australia became self-governing, the position was renamed Attorney-General. For two and a half years from 30 September 1857 to 9 May 1860, Richard Hanson was Premier. This was the time when Robert Torrens's Real Property Bill was going through, of which Hanson had initially an opponent.

He was appointed Chief Justice in November 1861 when Sir Charles Cooper could no longer support the continual obstruction of the court processes by second judge Benjamin Boothby. Boothby was horrified at a mere attorney being appointed direct from the bar above him, and for the next six years, continued to obstruct trials and insult his brother judges, Hanson and third judge Edward Gwynne. Boothby was finally removed by the Governor in 1867 in the middle of the famous Moonta Mines case, and the South Australian Supreme Court was able to slowly rebuild its severely damaged reputation.

Hanson had actually tolerated Boothby's jealous pedantry until 1863 when Boothby convinced Bishop Short of the Anglican Church and fifteen other colonists to boycott Hanson's wife from attending a ball at Government House. Hanson's wife had been his housekeeper before she married him and they had six children by this time. Governor Dominick Daly rebuked the bishop and named all the protesters in a report to London.

Hanson was more than a mere judge, he was a great jurist. He was a religious historian, and in 1875 published the 500 page *Apostle Paul and the Preaching of Christianity in the Primitive Church.* Later in his life he moved to a home near Mount Lofty and died there suddenly at the age of 71.

Hanson Chambers has remained a small set of chambers, but has been the address of a disproportionately large number of silks and judges. Over 80% of its occupants (16 out of 21 to 2020) have been appointed Queen's or Senior Counsel, and ten have been appointed to a superior court bench: Derek Bollen, John Doyle, Tim Anderson, Richard White, Tim Anderson, Kevin Nicholson, and Christopher Bleby to the Supreme Court of South Australia; Geoffrey Eames to the Supreme Court of Victoria, then its Court of Appeal; John Mansfield to the Federal Court and subsequently Richard White; and Michael Evans to Chief Judge of the District Court of South Australia.

Hanson Chambers members in 1998. Back: R J (Dick) Whitington, Richard White, Jonathan Wells, Timothy Stanley. Front: David Quick, Tim Anderson. (Rosey Boehm).

Hanson Chambers 2004. ABOVE. Standing: Kevin Nicholson, Margaret McPhee (clerk), Dick Whitington, Jonathan Wells, Jill Barnes (clerk), Timothy Stanley. Seated: Christopher Bleby, Richard White.

BELOW – in 2005. Standing: Timothy Stanley, Jill Barnes (clerk), Kevin Nicholson, Dick Whitington, Margaret McPhee (clerk), Jonathan Wells. Seated: Michael Evans, Christopher Bleby.

Late 1980s. Standing: John Doyle (now Solicitor–General), John Mansfield. Seated: Tim Anderson, Jonathan Wells.

Twenty years anniversary 1997: John Mansfield (Federal Court South Australia), John Doyle, (Chief Justice South Australia), Geoffrey Eames (Supreme Court Victoria).

Jeffcott Chambers

7 Gouger Street, Adelaide; 24 Flinders Street from March 2018
Opened: March 1982

Members in approximate order of joining:

Neil Lowrie	(1982–1985) DCSA
David Bleby	(1982–1997) SCSA
John von Doussa	(1982–1986) SCSA; FC
Bruce Lander	(1982–1994) SCSA; FC; ICAC
Robert Lawson	(1982– 1996)
Leonard Lindon	(1982)
Geoffrey Muecke	(1982–1999) DCSA
David Peek	(1982–1984)
Kelvyn Prescott	(1982–1985) MCSA
Malcolm Robertson	(1982–1996) DCSA
David Smith	(1982–1999) DCSA
Andrew Harris	(1982–
Edward Mullighan	(1982–1989) SCSA
Terence Worthington	(1984–1995) DCSA
Anthony Besanko	(1985–2001) SCSA; FC
Andrea Simpson	(1985–1998) DCSA
Martin Frayne	(1987–
David Lovell	(1990–2015)

Michael Manetta	(1995–
Carey Goodall	(1996–
Bernard Krupka	(1996–
Francis Stratford	(1996–
Anthony Crocker	(1997–
Simon Hanus	(1999–
Hugh Abbott	(1999–
Nicholas Swan	(1999–
Samuel Doyle	(2002–
Liesl Chapman	(2007–2012)
Peter Day	(2006–
Alan Lindsay	(2010–
Tom Besanko	(2012–
Nick Floreani	(2016–
Ian Robertson	(2018–
(Simon) Patrick O'Sullivan	(2008–2018) DCSA
Simon Ower	(2018–
Michael Barnett	(2018–
Anne Barnett	(2018–
Scott Evans	(2018–2020)
Penelope Kari	(2018–2019) FC
Paul Bullock	(2018–
Holly Veale	(2018–

Naomi Kereru	(2019–
Sam Ure	(2020–

In the early 1980s, as the independent bar continued to thrive, there was an increasing need for another set of chambers. After a meeting at the Stock Exchange Club Neil Lowrie, David Bleby QC and John von Doussa QC decided to found one. Their choice of building was an old burnt-out derelict hotel, earmarked for demolition by the State Government, right next to the old Supreme Court building.

The Supreme Court Hotel had been built of bluestone rubble in the 1870s and first granted a licence in 1875. So before it closed its doors in 1970, it had served the legal profession as an important independent bar of a different kind. After closing its doors as a pub, the State Government used it for offices for a few years, and then a fire destroyed its interior. By 1977 the Adelaide City Council decided to support a move to have it demolished.

Luckily this had not yet happened by the time Neil Lowrie had gathered support for a new chambers. Lowrie lobbied the Liberal government's Minister of Public Works, Dean Brown, in an effort to buy the building. Over the course of twelve months of negotiating, the government offered to lease the site. An initial ten year lease was set up, and to this day, Jeffcott Chambers remains leased from the South Australian State Government.

Sir John Jeffcott (1800–1837), South Australia's first Supreme Court judge. (JC)

The old hotel building was at this stage little more than a shell, and it took nine months and around $130,000 to restore it. Originally, the plan had been to sub-lease the ground floor to Butterworths. The government had not been happy about that, but during the construction period, another nine intending barristers were lined up ready to join the new chambers.

During this time as well, the need became obvious for a name for the new set of chambers. David Bleby rang Neil Lowrie late one night and suggested "Rumpole". But the pressure to name the chambers after a local identity won, and so an equally colourful character as Rumpole was chosen: Jeffcott. John Jeffcott (1800–1837) was South Australia's first judge, although he was only present for two or three separate periods during 1837, before he drowned at the end of the year.

In England Jeffcott had killed a man in a duel near Exeter, but had managed to avoid a conviction for murder. He also had accumulated a number of significant debts around the time he was appointed. Although he was supposed to have joined the team of inaugural dignitaries on the Buffalo, his creditors were waiting to arrest him at the port. He took another ship, the Isabella, secretly being rowed out at night. But the Isabella was going to Van Diemen's Land, and Jeffcott arrived there in January 1837. Unfortunately for South Australian justice at that time, in Tasmania he fell in love with his cousin Anne Kermode, and he did not arrive in South Australia until the end of April.

Jeffcott only sat on two trials. In between, he spent some more time

Supreme Court Hotel around 1890. (JC)

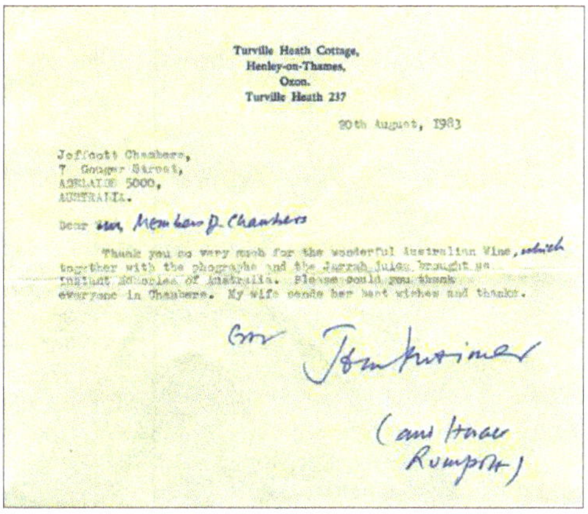

Turville Heath Cottage,
Henley-on-Thames,
Oxon.
Turville Heath 237

20th August, 1983

Jeffcott Chambers,
7 Gouger Street,
ADELAIDE 5000,
AUSTRALIA.

Dear Members of Chambers

Thank you so very much for the wonderful Australian Wine, which together with the photographs and the Jarrah Juice brought us instant memories of Australia. Please could you thank everyone in Chambers. My wife sends her best wishes and thanks.

Love John Mortimer

(and Horace Rumpole)

John Mortimer's subsequent letter of thanks, dated 20 August 1983. (JC)

(Left) John Mortimer visiting Jeffcott Chambers in 1983. (JC)

in Tasmania with his fiancée. In December 1837, on another voyage to go and see her, he drowned in a storm at the mouth of the River Murray, and his body was never recovered. Despite his short stay in the nascent province, he managed to get both his name and that of his fiancée on streets in North Adelaide. Ralph Hague published a biography of Jeffcott which is available in the University of Adelaide's Barr Smith Library.

Rumpole was not forgotten. The company that holds the lease and manages Jeffcott Chambers is Rumpole Pty Ltd. Neil Lowrie wrote to John Mortimer and asked him for approval to use the name, and invited him to visit. The author was very pleased and visited in 1983 and signed the wall in the library.

Soon after Jeffcott Chambers was open Kate Jennings joined the office staff. Kate's approach to inquiries from solicitors was not to allow them to leave or hang up without disgorging a brief. Work flowed in. Andrew Harris, the youngest member, had joined expecting only initially to get research work from Queens' Counsel such as John von Doussa. He found that he was receiving briefs from the first week and never did any research.

Andrew Harris went on to get silk, joining the ten of the twelve founding members who either were silks at the beginning, or were appointed since. John von Doussa and Bruce Lander were appointed judges not only to the South Australian Supreme Court, but subsequently the Federal Court. Bruce Lander was South Australia's first Independent Commissioner Against Corruption. Robert Lawson became more and more involved in his political career, and was Attorney-General in 2001–2002. Patrick O'Sullivan was appointed to the District Court of South Australia in 2018 and Penelope Kari to the Federal Circuit Court of Australia (Adelaide) in 2019.

After the State Government took back the building to expand the courts, the members of Jeffcott Chambers moved to 24 Flinders Street. Apart from having much more room – 21 barristers in 2020 – the building had once been the location of the Crown Prosecutor's Office.

Kate Jennings retired as Clerk of Chambers in 2005. The Clerks of Chambers since have been Trish Sced from 2005, Tricia Fehlberg from 2016 and Christine Salvemini from 2020.

Members of Jeffcott Chambers around 1985. (Coming down the stairs) David Peek, David Bleby, David Smith, Geoffrey Muecke, Anthony Besanko, Malcolm Robertson, Andrea Simpson, Andrew Harris. (L–R) Robert Lawson, Neil Lowrie, David Lovett, Terry Worthington, John von Doussa, Bruce Lander. (JC)

Members of Jeffcott Chambers around 2020. Back row L–R Martin Frayne, Hugh Abbott, Ben Krupka, Carey Goodall, Paul Bullock, Michael Barnett, Tom Besanko, Anthony Crocker, Scott Evans. Front row L–R Nicholas Swan, Simon Ower, Anne Barnett, Ian Robertson, Penelope Kari, Simon Hanus, Holly Veale, Peter Day, Christine Salvemini, Tricia Fehlberg, Ella Cameron, Andrew Harris. Absent: Alan Lindsay, Nicholas Floreani. (JC)

Libra Chambers

(Cleland Chambers from 1997)
27 Waterfall Gully Road, Beaumont
Opened: 1973; closed: 2002

Members in approximate order of joining:

Pamela Cleland	(1973–1993)
Kevin Borick	(1973–2002)
David Chapman	(1978–ca 1991)
Gary Hevey	(1993–2000)
Patricia Knutson	(1997–2000)

Pam Cleland had been running a busy law practice from two buildings on her property at 27 Waterfall Gully Road for nine years when she and Kevin Borick signed the bar roll in 1973 and committed to practise only as barristers. Pam Cleland therefore is the first female barrister to join the independent bar, and Kevin Borick was eventually appointed silk in 1999. They worked from chambers Pam had built in 1966 which was christened Libra Chambers, and Libra therefore was South Australia's second set of chambers.

The first building Pam had built in 1964, Azalea House, remained a mixed barrister–solicitor practice and its early occupants were Margaret Nyland, Piers Plumridge and David Haines. In 1997, after Margaret Nyland was appointed to the Supreme Court, she returned to open the renamed Cleland Chambers. The lawyers out at Azalea House and Libra Chambers dealt with many divorce and criminal cases, and Pam believed that her luxurious foothills setting soothed the nerves of her stressed clients.

Pam Cleland obtained an Arts degree and also painted, studying for a while under Geoffrey Smart. She only enrolled in law later as it was the cheapest course at the University of Adelaide. She had no intention of practising, but Roma Mitchell persuaded her and took on Cleland's articles. She was admitted in 1957 and went to work for Genders Wilson and Bray. The firm was based in Shakespeare Chambers, now a backpackers hostel, on

Pam Cleland, first female to sign the bar roll, with Margaret Nyland on her birthday in the late 1980s. (courtesy Margaret Nyland)

Waymouth Street. That same year Bray took silk and Cleland became his regular junior. She was one of the very few women in the legal profession at the time, and if that was not sufficient for her to stand out, she painted her office bright yellow with purple skirtings, and filled it with plants and an aquarium.

Some years later, Cleland appeared before her old articles principal, now the Honourable Justice Mitchell. Her Honour adjourned and called counsel into her chambers where etiquette decreed they remove their wigs. Cleland had recently shaved her head after tiring of long bleached-blond hair and out of court wore a natural-style wig while it grew back. But when robing as counsel she took this wig off and replaced it with the horsehair wig so as not to wear two wigs at the same time. She did not have time to return to the robing room when summonsed to Roma Mitchell's chambers where she politely removed her court wig.

Wellington Chambers

211 Wellington Square, North Adelaide
Open: 1982–1986

Members in approximate order of joining:

Michael Abbott	(1982–1986)
Gordon Barrett	(1984–1986)
Barry Jennings	(1984–1986)
John Lyons	(1984–1986)
Marie Shaw	(1984–1986)
Simon Stretton	(1982–1986)

Michael Abbott QC is one of Adelaide's most prominent barristers and one of the small number whose reputation is known to the general public. He has practised as a sole practitioner since his admission in March 1966, acting as Counsel before joining the independent bar on a number of Royal Commissions, early ones including the Vietnam Moratorium and the sacking of Police Commissioner Harold Salisbury.

After joining the independent bar in 1982, Michael Abbott established Wellington Chambers with Simon Stretton. The practical problem that presented itself – as it does with all the suburban practices – is lack of proximity to the city courts and parking difficulties. Thus four years later Wellington Chambers relocated to 21 Market Street. All the barristers moved to the new address except Marie Shaw who went to Rose Park Chambers. Market Street eventually moved and became Mitchell Chambers.

Other members of chambers included John Harrison, Geoffrey Eames, David Peek and Richard Hogan. Mary Davidge was clerk of chambers and her entrepreneurial approach helped get briefs.

Market Street Chambers

21 Market Street, Adelaide
Open: 1986–1991

Members in approximate order of joining:

Michael Abbott	(1986–1990)
Gordon Barrett	(1986–1991)
Barry Jennings	(1986–1991)
John Lyons	(1986–1991)
Simon Stretton	(1986–1991)
William Braithwaite	(1986–1991)
Christopher Cocks	(1986–1989)
James Telfer	(1986–1991)
Hugh Abbott	(1987–1991)
Fazio di Fazio	(1987–1991)
Susan O'Connor	(1987–1991)
Anthony Possingham	(1987–1991)
Mark Rice	(1987–1991)
Ross Mayne	(1990–1991)
William Retalic	(1990–1991)
Marie Shaw	(1989–1991)

Rose Park Chambers

297 Fullarton Road, Rose Park
Open: 1982–2002

Members in approximate order of joining:

(Eleanor) Frances Nelson	(1982–1990); (1995–2002)
Mark Pickhaver	(1985–1990)
Greg Holland	(1985–1990)
Marie Shaw	(1987–1989)
Ian Polson	(1988–1993)
Gary Coppola	(1998)

Torrens Chambers

Opened: 1984 in 11th Floor, 185 Victoria Square;
moved to 78 Angas Street in July 1990; 61–63 Carrington Street

Members in approximate order of joining:

Darrell Trim	(1984–2018)
Stephen Dowd	(1984–1989)
Timothy Bryant	(1984–)[1]
Timothy Jackson	(1984–1987)
Paul Gabrynowicz	(1985–1989)
Richard Mellows	(1984–
Rosemary Colton	(1985–1994)
Michael Bell	(1987–)
Brian Baillie	(1988–1996)
Mark Clisby	(1990–1991)
Michael Evans	(1991–1994)
Ian Polson	(1991–1994)
Paul Gabrynowicz	(1993–1995)
Nicholas Swan	(1993–1999)
Bernard O'Brien	(1994–)
Roger Sallis	(1994–2000)
John Keen	(1995–)

1 Some updated information was not available at time of publication.

Andrew Moffa	(1995–1996)
Andrew Tokley	(1997–2008)
Helena Jasinski	(1998–2000)
Henry Heuzenroeder	(2000–2013)
Andrew Jones	(2002–)
David Crocker	(2004–2014)
Matthew Young	(2012–
Geoffrey Britton	(2013–
Cheryl Smith	(2013–

Tim Bryant joined the independent bar in early 1983 and practised for a year on the seventh floor at 185 Victoria Square –known then as the MLC Centre and later as Beacon House. At the same time Stephen Dowd and his firm S J Dowd & Co. shared the eleventh floor with the building's caretaker. Stephen Dowd was also planning to join the independent bar, and when in early 1984 the caretaker's premises next to his offices was permanently vacated he saw an opportunity to take the space.

Sir Robert Torrens painted by John Upton ca. 1880. (NLA)

He approached Tim Bryant and the two discussed the advantages of practising from a set of chambers rather than on a sole basis. They approached Darrell Trim, who was a partner in the firm of Straffords and Tim Jackson who was working for Wallmans. Torrens Chambers opened on 1 July 1984 on the eleventh floor of 185 Victoria Square.

The chambers diverged from the nascent custom of taking judges' names. Sir Robert Richard Torrens (1814–1884) was not a lawyer, nevertheless he was responsible for the successful establishment in South Australia of the much simplified system of recording land ownership that is now found worldwide.

Torrens appears to have been a single–minded antagonist who took up the already existing land titles registration crusade in 1856, the year after he became a member of the Executive Council. Other supporters along the way included future Chief Justice Richard Hanson. It was Torrens who took up the cause with the zeal it needed to get the necessary bills passed through the nascent South Australian parliament. Once the legislation was enacted in 1858, he resigned from parliament and took up the challenge of putting it into practice as Registrar-General.

Torrens was the son of Colonel Robert Torrens, who was the chairman of the colonisation commission for South Australia. The river that flows through Adelaide is named after the Colonel, not his son. Sir Robert, the land titles reformer, moved to England in 1865 and tried to introduce his system there, but without success. He lived the rest of his life in Devon. Because of the creation of the land broker in South Australia, solicitors there have not had conveyancing as their bread and butter, as in other states. So Robert Torrens's legacy was not just a better system of land titles, but also a considerably smaller legal profession. In July 1990, Torrens Chambers moved into an old building which had begun life as the Old Colonist Hotel in 1864, and was later known as the Angas Hotel. As of 2020, it is located at 61–63 Carrington Street.

Members of Torrens Chambers in 1998. Back: Roger Sallis, Nicholas Swan, Richard Mellows, Andrew Tokley, John Keen. Seated: Helena Jasinski, Darrell Trim, Tim Bryant. (Rosey Boehm)

Bateson's rendition of members of Torrens Chambers. Middle: Helena Jasinski. Left Group: (Top two) Richard Mellows, Michael Evans. (L–R) Roger Sallis, Brian Baillie, Tim Bryant, Tim Jackson, Darrell Trim. Right Group: (Top two) Nicholas Swan, Rosemary Colton. (L–R) Michael Bell, Ian Poulson, John Keen, Paul Gabrynowicz, Bernard O'Brien. (Darrell Trim)

Campbell Chambers

Opened: 1984 at 118 King William Street;
1995 at 22 Grenfell Street; 2004 at 360 King William Street;
From August 2017: 113 Carrington Street

Members in approximate order of joining:

Steven Strickland	(1984–1999) Family Court
Geoffrey Noble	(1984–
Robert Park	(1984–1985)
Neville Morcombe	(1985–2000)
Gary Hevey	(1985–1987)
John Cummins	(1986–1994)
Philip McNamara	(1986–1995)
Craig McCarthy	(1989–1995)
Ross Richards	(1994–
Christine Mead	(1995–1999)
John Morcombe	(1995–2006) Federal Magistrate
David Berman	(1995–2013) Family Court
Edward Jolly	(1998–1999)
Stuart Lindsay	(1998–1999)
Catherine Jeffries	(1999–2004)
Brian McQuade	(1999–2005)
Margaret Ross	(2000–
Andrew Moffa	(2000–2017)

David Whittle	(2003–2014) Magistrate
Tom Birchall	(ca 2008–2016)
John Dillon	(left 2018)
Noelle Hurley	(?)
Peter Heinrich	(left 2017; 2020–
Jayne Basheer	(left 2015) Magistrate
Penelope Kari	(2010–2018)
Mark Anderson	(left 2020)
Daniel Praolini	(2018–

Steven Strickland and Geoffrey Noble established the first family court chambers in 1984. The third barrister, Robert Park, was not a family court lawyer, however, and ever since Campbell Chambers has always housed barristers who practised in other areas.

Strickland and Noble were aware of the nascent trend of naming chambers after State judges, but opted for an early contributor to the development of divorce law. Lord John Campbell (1779–1861) was the son of a minister in Fife, Scotland, who joined Lincoln's Inn around the turn of the nineteenth century. According to Anthony Mockler in *Lions under the Throne* (London: Frederick Muller, 1983) Campbell's career at the bar was nothing outstanding. But when he was forty he married Mary Scarlett, which was supposed to be the best thing he ever did.

His father–in–law, Sir James Scarlett, became Attorney–General in 1827 and immediately appointed John Campbell a King's Counsel. From then on his career continued in leaps and bounds. Campbell entered parliament and was himself Attorney-General from 1834 to 1841. In the 1840s and 1850s he published the best–selling seven-volume series on the Lord Chief Justices of England – some being published when he was Lord Chief Justice – 1850 –1859.

In the House of Commons Campbell was associated with legal reforms in the areas of real estate and local government, and he organised the investigating commissions and guided the bills through Parliament. He was directly responsible for the Libel Act (1843), the Copyright Act (1846), and the Obscene Publications Act (1857). Campbell was a friend of Charles Dickens, and it may have been through the great novelist that the politician came to understand the problems of getting a divorce for poor people. Divorces were practically impossible to get for them.

He tried for many years to get a divorce reform bill through parliament but it was not until he had left in 1857 and was Lord Chief Justice that the "Act to amend the Law relating to Divorce and Matrimonial Causes in England" was finally passed. Nevertheless, Lord Campbell was responsible for this landmark legislation which allowed divorces for anyone without regard to their class.

His energy never left him. In 1859 he was appointed Lord Chancellor at almost eighty years old. He died just two years later, but only after a day sitting in court, a cabinet meeting, walking home, writing a judgment, having a dinner party, and finally working in his study, where his valet found him next morning dead in his chair.

Members of Campbell Chambers in 1998. (L–R) David Berman, Ross Richards, Steve Strickland, John Morcombe, Geoff Noble, Neville Morcombe. (Seated) Christine Mead. (Rosey Boehm)

Edmund Barton Chambers

72 Wright Street, Adelaide
Opened: 1 November 1987

Members in approximate order of joining:

Paul Cuthbertson	(1987–2009) DCSA
David Greenwell	(1987–1996)
David Haines	(1987–2005)
Mark Rice	(1989–1994) DCSA
Paul Rice	(1989–1998) DCSA
Neville Rochow	(1989–1992)
Marie Shaw	(1989–2004) Legal Services, DCSA
Sydney Tilmouth	(1989–2005) DCSA
Michael Boylan	(1990–2004) DCSA
Christopher Kourakis	(1990–2003) Solicitor-General; SCSA 2008; Chief Justice 2012
Barry Beazley	(1992–2004) DCSA
Stephen Walsh	(1992–
Jonathon Hyde	(1997–2002)
Arlene MacDonald	(1996–2013)
David Chapman	(1997)
Patrick O'Sullivan	(1997–2018) DCSA
Rosemary Davey	(1998–2007) DCSA (dec.)
Barry Jenner	(1998–2003)

Michael Ward	(1999–2001)
William Boucaut	(1998–2010)
Edward Jolly	(1999–2005)
Mark Livesey	(2002–2003)
Neville Morcombe	(2002–
Anthony Schapel	(2001–2005) Deputy Coroner
Simon Ower	(2002–2018)
Sophie David	(2003–2009) DCSA 2015
Alexander Ward	(2003–
Tom Duggan	(2004–2012)
Liesl Chapman	(2005–2008) DCSA 2017
Scott Henchliffe	(2005–
Darren Blight	(2005–2014)
Jo-anne Deuter	(2005–2006) DCSA 2019
Michael Mills	(2005–
Mark O'Loughlin	(2006–2010)
Anthony Durkin	(2006–2012)
Martin Anders	(2007–
Nick Floreani	(2008–2016)
Greg King	(2008–2011)
Stephen Apps	(2008–2020)
Michael Manetta	(2009–2012)
Tim Heffernan	(2010–2015) FCCA

Edward Stratton-Smith	(2010–
David Crocker	(2014–
Tony Hurren	(2014–
Heath Barklay	(2015–
Ian Thomas	(2014–2016)
Scott Evans	(2015–2017)
Noelle Hurley	(2015–2018)
Candida D'Arcy	(2015–
Chad Jacobi	(2016–
Ben Armstrong	(2017–
Holly Stanley	(2016–2017)
Mark Taylor	(2018–
Marita Pangallo	(2018–2019)
Christian Munt	(2018–
Adam Kimber	(2019–2020) DCSA
Kathryn Waite	(2019–
Lauren Gavranich	(2019–
Mardi Conduit	(2019–
Brad McCloud	(2020–
Chris Kummerow	(2020–

The genesis of Edmund Barton Chambers was a meeting at a café in Flinders Street in 1987. Present were Paul Cuthbertson, David Greenwell, David Haines and Sydney Tilmouth. The set of chambers that resulted, which had no name at this stage, first set up at 82 Franklin Street. Later, Neville Rochow joined the group and the search for a new address began. There was an empty sandstone building at 72 Wright Street, and two newcomers, Paul and Mark Rice, paid $20,000 for an option to purchase the building.

The move to the new address took place in 1989, and the set of chambers has grown to house seventeen barristers. From this period, the chambers named itself after Australia's first prime minister, Edmund Barton (1849–1920). His first notable achievement had been in 1883, when at 34 he became Speaker in the New South Wales parliament. By this time he was also an ardent supporter of federating the Australian colonies into a nation. He was a regular speaker at the conventions that took place over the 1890s.

After a term as Attorney-General of New South Wales from 1891 to 1894, Barton campaigned full–time for Federation, and became its acknowledged leader. He resigned from the New South Wales parliament in February 1900, and the next month went to London as leader of the Australian delegation to explain the constitution to the Imperial government.

Barton was nevertheless not the first choice for the new nation's first prime minister. It was rumoured that he would most likely be the first Chief Justice of the High Court. But when Sir William Lyne – who had been an opponent of Federation – failed to form its first ministry, Barton was asked and he succeeded. In September 1903, Edmund resigned as prime minister and joined the new High Court as its first senior puisne judge.

The building at 72 Wright Street which houses Edmund Barton Chambers was built originally as a church for the deaf.

Mid 2000s: Front seated: Anthony Schapel, Sophie David, Alexander Ward, Neville Morcombe. Rear standing: Tom Duggan, Arlene Macdonald, Edward Jolly, Simon Ower, Di Dawson (Clerk of Chambers), Samantha Carter (Clerk), William Boucaut, Denise Ardlie (Clerk), Michael Boylan, Paul Cuthbertson, Rosemary Davey. (Bruce Weir)

Around 2016: Front row: Edward Stratton-Smith, Chad Jacobi, Patrick O'Sullivan, Neville Morcombe, Martin Anders, Michael Mills.
Back row: Alexander Ward, Stephen Walsh, David Crocker, Noelle Hurley, Anthony Hurren, Candida D'Arcy, Scott Henchliffe, Heath Barklay, Simon Ower, Scott Evans. (absent Stephen Apps) (EBC)

Murray Chambers

12 Coglin Street, Adelaide
Opened: 1984

Members in approximate order of joining:

Richard Halliday	(1984–
Anthony Besanko	(1984–1985)
John Costello	(1984–2010)
Peter Eriksen	(1984–2013)
Brian Hayes	(1984–
Denys Simpson	(1985–1987; 2006–2008)
Brian Martin	(1985–1995) SCSA 1999
Mark Blumberg	(1986–2010)
Richard Evans	(1987–2001)
Robyn Layton	(1990–2005) SCSA
Philip McNamara	(1995–
Simon Milazzo	(1990–2006)
David Peek	(1990–2010) SCSA
Rauf Soulio	(1990–2006) DCSA
Helena Jasinski	(1990–1997)
Nicole Symons	(1997–1999)
Sashi Maharaj	(1999–2016)
John Rau	(1998–2010; 2018–) AGSA, Dep. Premier

Andrew Collett	(2000–2017)
Mark Roberts	(2002–
Peter Quinn	(2005–
Thomas Cox	(2005–2011)
Arturo Dal Cin	(2006–
Kerry Clark	(2008–
Gillian Walker	(2010–
Philip Adams	(2010–
Shane Spence	(2010–2014)
Taruna Heuzenroeder	(2011–
Mark Douglas	(2011–
Bernard Walrut	(2011–
James McMillan	(2014–2019)
Andrew Schatz	(2016–
Daniella Di Girolamo	(2018–2019)
Sally Heidenriech	(2019–
Michelle Hamlyn	(2019–
Henry Heuzenroeder	(2013–
Katarina Grenfell	(2018–
Peter Barnes	(2018–
Darrell Trim	(2018–
Tim Kentish	(2020–

One impetus for the founding of Murray Chambers was Brian Hayes's decision to leave Norman Waterhouse and join the independent bar. He asked Anthony Besanko if he would like to replace him, but Besanko was also thinking of joining the independent bar. At a Christmas party in 1983, Brian Hayes and Peter Eriksen discussed setting up their own chambers, and that very night saw a "For Lease" sign on 12 Coglin Street.

The bluestone building which was originally a funeral parlour was rented initially, and seven barristers with a range of specialisations began practising in 1984. Catherine Branson had also been ready to join, but at the last minute, was appointed Crown Solicitor. The set of chambers was named after the State's fourth Chief Justice Sir George John Robert Murray (1863–1942), and rescued him from the almost total oblivion into which he had fallen since his death.

Sir George Murray and his Associate G G Noble around the late 1930s. (*Advertiser*)

Murray's father had been a wealthy pastoralist and Merino sheep breeder, and one of his house-guests the year George was born was John McDouall Stuart (1815–1866) who had just returned from his epic journey as the first European to cross Australia through the centre from Adelaide to Darwin. George Murray and his siblings went to school in Scotland as well as in Adelaide. Later, Murray did a laws degree at Trinity College, Cambridge, after receiving his Bachelor of Arts from the University of Adelaide.

Except for a number of voyages to Britain and New Zealand, Murray never left the family home at Magill. He lived there with his sister Margaret and both died unmarried. When Murray was appointed to the Supreme Court of South Australia in 1912, he became the first judge to hold a laws degree, and no judge appointed since has not had one. In 1916, he replaced Samuel Way as Chief Justice, Lieutenant-Governor and Chancellor of the University of Adelaide.

Murray inherited money from a number of his relatives and was able to make generous donations to the University of Adelaide, including from his estate after death totalling around 140,000 pounds. That sum in 1942 when he died was 56 times the amount of the Chief Justice's annual salary. He also donated 10,000 pounds to allow the Law Society to have a library for the use of all practitioners, given the increasing cost and number of law reports being published.

The members of Murray Chambers purchased their building in 1989 and added six new chambers. The extension was built from the bluestone from the old shed at the back in Mill Street that was demolished, thus preserving the integrity of the original building.

Murray Chambers has 20 full members as of the publication of this edition, of whom 7 are female.

Original members of Murray Chambers. STANDING: Peter Eriksen, Jack Costello, Brian Hayes, Richard Halliday. SEATED: Denys Simpson, Richard Evans, Anthony Besanko. (MC)

Murray Chambers in 2018. (MC)

Members of Murray Chambers ca 1995. STANDING: Richard Evans, Philip McNamara, Mark Blumberg, Simon Milazzo, Richard Halliday, Peter Eriksen, Rauf Soulio, Jack Costello, David Peek. SEATED: Helena Jasinski, Brian Hayes, Robyn Layton, Brian Martin. (MC)

Clerks of Chambers 1984–2004: Luba Turner, Eileen West, Deborah Dearman, Dianne Posch, Barbara Dudson. (MC)

Members of Murray Chambers at the Bar Dinner in 2019: (left to right, standing then seated) Gillian Walker, Michelle Hamlyn, Kerry Clark, Mark Roberts, Mark Douglas, Sally Heidenreich, Peter Barnes, Peter Quinn, Philip Adams, Katarina Grenfell, Brian Hayes. (MC)

Kingston Chambers

47 Wright Street
Opened: 1 January 1989, closed[1]

Members in approximate order of joining:

Geoffrey Britton	(1989–)
Christopher Cocks	(1989–1995)
Stuart Cole	(1989–2001)
Ross Richards	(1989–1993)
David Howard	(1989–)
Terence McRae	(1991–)
Grant Germein	(1997–1998)
Martin Keith	(1997–2001)
Brian Austin	(2002–)
Sean Richter	(2002–2010)
Graham Dart	(2003–)

1 Updated information was not available at time of publication

Geoffrey Britton and Stuart Cole were practising from premises in Peel Street, and Christopher Cocks – one time occupant of Bar Chambers and magistrate – from Market Street Chambers when they decided to form Kingston Chambers.

Charles Cameron Kingston (1850–1908) was one of the most explosive politicians in Australian history. He held the record term of six years as premier (1893–1899) before it was broken by Thomas Playford. During that period he warred constantly with a variety of people in diverse areas.

Even when he was elected premier in June 1893, he was still on a 12-month good behaviour bond for organising a duel in Victoria Square. That was his response for being called "a coward, a bully and a disgrace to the legal profession" by Sir Richard Baker, a conservative member of the Legislative Council. Two years later – he would be premier for four more – as he entered the corner of Grote Street and Victoria Square, he was struck on the neck by Henry Sparks, the manager of the South Australian Company, with a horsewhip. Kingston had offended Sparks with some remarks he had made at a workers' meeting in Port Pirie. Kingston reacted violently and passers–by had to break up the fist fight that followed. By coincidence, his statue in Victoria Square gazes defiantly over the spot where this otherwise long-forgotten scuffle took place.

Statue of Charles Kingston in Victoria Square, Adelaide. (KC)

Kingston was responsible for illegally detaining a political opponent in Parkside Lunatic Asylum in 1898 for four months. In 1896 Paris Nesbit QC had stood as a candidate for the seat of Barossa and inflamed the premier by encouraging electors to "thrust Kingston's great fat unwieldy despotic carcass on to the Opposition benches". Kingston won that election but, according to Graham Loughlin, did not forget his former friend's torrent of abuse.

Paris Nesbit occasionally spent periods in psychiatric care as a result of his otherwise brilliant legal career being punctuated by bouts of psychosis. He was in already in Parkside asylum when Kingston pounced. Kingston held a special cabinet meeting and sent Dr Cleland, the medical superintendent at

Members of Kingston Chambers around 1998: Terence McRae, Grant Germein, Stuart Cole, Geoffrey Britton, David Howard, Christopher Cocks, Martin Keith. (Rosey Boehm)

Below: Kingston Chambers on Wright Street. (KC)

Above: (Standing) Geoffrey Britton, Grant Germein, Christopher Cocks, Stuart Cole, Martin Keith. (Sitting) David Howard, Terence McCrae. (Rosey Boehm)

Below, after 2003: Brian Austin, Graham Dart, David Howard, Geoffrey Britton, Terence McRae, Sean Richter. (KC)

Parkside a memo which ordered that: "Mr Nesbit must not be released on any pretext whatever without Ministerial authority". This directive was entirely illegal and effectively made Nesbit a political prisoner. Four months later Justice Bundey ordered his immediate release.

From 1894 until 1899 – all but the first year of Charles Kingston's premiership – an ongoing dispute raged between his government, the Adelaide Hospital board and hospital staff. By January 1898, 92 people had either resigned or been dismissed, including at one time the entire board. The total included: "17 Honorary Medical staff, 2 Medical Superintendents, a senior Resident Physician, 6 Junior Medical Officers, 20 members of the Board of Management. 2 Superintendents of Nurses, 2 Superintendents of Night Nurses, 11 Charge Nurses, 3 Probationers, 5 Wardsmaids, a Needlewoman, 2 Assistant Dispensers, a Messenger and 19 medical students".

Kingston's antagonistic personality appears to have fueled the entire dispute from beginning to end. By the mid–1890s, the surgeons as a group refused to work at the hospital and from 1897 to 1900 medicine could not be taught at the University of Adelaide. Kingston had to lure two surgeons from England – one was Leith Napier, father of Chief Justice Mellis Napier.

Kingston was a powerful force in the federation movement and secured the entry of South Australia into the Federal Council of Australia when he had been attorney–general in 1888. He helped draft the federal constitution, and he would be the new nation's first Minister of Trade and Customs. But Kingston's intense work schedule as a Commonwealth minister and law partner took its toll on his health. In July 1903 he resigned, ostensibly because Cabinet wanted to alter a clause in a Bill he had publicly committed himself to. Yet he had been earmarked to take over as Prime Minister when Edmund Barton stepped down. The real reason was that his health was deteriorating rapidly. He returned briefly to State politics and Alfred Deakin took over from Barton instead.

Kingston's left two enduring legacies to his day – one of which was the federal constitution. The other is perhaps even more important. In 1893, he gave women the vote, and the 1896 state election was the first in which South Australian women turned up at the polling booths. New Zealand women had beaten them to be the first in the world, having already voted in the country's 1893 election.

John Bray Chambers

142 Wright Street, Adelaide;
84 Sturt Street from 2013
Opened: 1990

Members in approximate order of joining:

Gregory Holland	(1990–2013)
Eleanor (Frances) Nelson	(1990–1995)
Mark Pickhaver	(1990–2012)
Maurine Pyke	(1991–
Richard Hogan	(1996–2003)
Diana Dibden	(1997–2002)
Julian Hicks	(1996–2013)
Louise Bedson	(2001–2002)
Mark Grogan	(1998–2002)
Holly Leeson	(2001–2003)
Patrick Liptak	(2003–2013)
Adele du Barry	(2004–2013)
Mark Boehm	(2006–2013)
Dora Fuda	(ca 2007–2013)
Andrea Horvath	(ca 2007–2013)
Vanessa Lee	(ca 2007–2013)
Mark Anderson	(ca 2007–2013)
Lesley Hastwell	(2015–2017)

John Bray Chambers was established in 1990 by the three barristers occupying Rose Park Chambers, Frances Nelson, Mark Pickhaver and Gregory Holland. It was the first set of chambers to be named after a living legal luminary, and John Bray therefore was available to open them.

Bray was one of Australia's most gifted jurists. When he was twenty-five he became the second, and as it turned out, the last person to be awarded a Doctor of Laws for a thesis from the University of Adelaide. He did not believe in specialising and his career as a barrister spread over all the jurisdictions. One of his great triumphs in crime was in *R v Howe* (1958–59) 100 CLR 448. Bray trawled back to 1640 to find authorities that supported his argument that when the force used in self-defence was sufficiently excessive to kill the aggressor, the appropriate conviction should be manslaughter not murder. His client was sent to prison, better nevertheless than hanging.

John Bray (1912–1995) outside his home at 39 Hurtle Square, Adelaide. (*Advertiser*)

Bray was fearless enough to appear against the government in *R v Rivett* in 1960. The trial was the backlash of the Stuart affair. The Playford government sued the editor of the Adelaide News on nine separate accounts of seditious and defamatory libel for some headlines announcing the abrupt resignation of Jack Shand QC. Playford believed that the headlines libelled Chief Justice Sir Mellis Napier, who had been the Royal Commissioner investigating the Stuart trial and appeals.

Bray's triumphant defence had consequences. Later, in 1967, Police Commissioner McKinna tried to dissuade Don Dunstan from appointing John Bray as Chief Justice to replace Napier by showing him some secret surveillance reports of Bray's social life. Dunstan showed them to Bray, who noticed that they dated from the time he was defending Rohan Rivett. Despite reading dozens of books a week aside from the needs of his legal research, Bray hardly needed any sleep. He often stayed out until two or three in the morning on week nights and then walked home – on more than one occasion arousing the interest of passing police patrols. Needless to say, there was no legal reason that the police should have been watching John Bray.

Bray became an outstanding Chief Justice and is the first South Australian judge to be cited by the Privy Council. He also published seven volumes of poetry and a biography of third-century Roman emperor Galienus. He was on the State Library board for forty years and was a foundation member of the Adelaide Festival board. While Chief Justice, he presented readings of his poetry at Writers' Weeks and also at the opening of the Festival Theatre in 1976.

Bray Chambers members in 2004 when Maurine Pyke took silk. ABOVE: Standing: Richard Hogan, Di Dibden, Mark Pickhaver, Maurine Pyke. Seated: Julian Hicks.

ABOVE: L-R: Angela Ferdinandy, Maureen Pyke, Greg Holland, Adele du Barry.

Mitchell Chambers

27 Surflen Street, Adelaide
Opened: 1991

Members in approximate order of joining:

Hugh Abbott	(1991–1999)
Grant Algie	(1991–2017)
Gordon Barrett	(1991–2005)
Fazio de Fazio	(1991–)[1]
John Lyons	(1991–)
Ross Mayne	(1991–2001)
Anthony Possingham	(1991–
William Retalic	(1991–)
Simon Stretton	(1991–2005)
Christopher Swan	(1991–1995)
James Telfer	(1991–)
Gabrielle Brown	(1995–)
Malcolm Gray	(1995–2000) ACT SC
Michael Saies	(1996–)
Michael Doyle	(2001–
Shane Spence	(2003–)
John White	(2005
Sean Richter	(2010–2014)

1 Some information was not available by time of printing.

Gilbert Aitken	(2007–
Josephine Battiste	(2016–
Liz Bowering	(2020–
Alison James	(2019–
Robert Kane	(2013–
Leanne Larosa	(2018–
Craig Lind	(2018–
Michael Tilley	(2019–

Mitchell Chambers is one of the sets of chambers that evolved rather than was founded from new. It can trace its origins to Wellington Chambers, founded in 1982 with two barristers: Michael Abbott and Simon Stretton, which quickly grew.

In 1986 the group moved to 21 Market Street to be closer to the courts and was renamed Market Street Chambers. Five years later the chambers split up but a group looked for chambers elsewhere. The building chosen on Surflen Street had been built around 1926 for a luggage factory. It was subsequently used as a bank's storage area, then divided with an office for an architect in one half, and a lighting retailer in the other.

With a new address and a membership of ten, the chambers were named after Dame Roma Mitchell, who was governor of South Australia when she opened them. Dame Roma's most enduring impact on the legal profession in Australia was to break through the men–only barrier at the top. She was the first female in Australia to be appointed to Queen's Counsel in 1962 and the first Australian female Supreme Court judge appointed in 1965. After she retired in 1983, she was appointed the first Australian female Chancellor (University of Adelaide), and was the first female Australian Governor in 1990.

Roma Mitchell had a strong commitment to social justice and she believed that the law was one way to achieve that. From 1970 until 1981 she headed the South Australian Criminal Law and Penal Methods Reform Committee which produced five reports containing 907 recommendations.

She was also chair of the Parole Board from 1974 until 1981. That year she became the founding chair of the Commission for Human Rights.

ABOVE. Mitchell Chambers ca 1998. Standing: Fazio de Fazio, William Retalic, Anthony Possingham, John Lyons, Grant Algie, Simon Stretton, Hugh Abbott, Michael Saies, Gabby Brown. Seated: Malcolm Gray, Dame Roma Mitchell, Gordon Barrett. (Rosey Boehm)

Anthony Mason Chambers

201 Victoria Square since 2006
Opened as Divett Chambers at 22 Divett Place in February 1993;
opened at Victoria Square on 20 October 2006 by Sir Anthony Mason

Members in approximate order of joining:

Tom Birchall	(1993–2015)
Paul Heywood-Smith	(1993–
David Wicks	(1993–1998) SCSA
Paul Slattery	(1994–2012) DCSA
Russel Harms	(1996–
Richard Ross-Smith	(1996–
David Riggall	(2002–
Alex Lazarevich	(2004–
Vickie Chapman	(2006–
Claire O'Connor	(2006–2015)
Jo-Anne Deuter	(2006–2019) DCSA
Natalie Charlesworth	(2007–2013) FCA 2016–
Andrew Tokley	(2008–
Michael Manetta	(2008–2009)
Mark Anderson	(2009–2014)
Stephen Mitchell	(2010–
Paul Bullock	(2012–2018)
David Blyth	(2014–2020)

Martin Hoile	(2015–
Matt Murphy	(2015–
Maria Demosthenous	(2016–2018)
Eliza Bergin	(2017–
Audrey Bosboom	(2019–
Lewis Gentry	(2019–2020)
(Edward) Ted Guthrie	(2016–2020)
Marissa Mackie	(2020–
Matoula Makris	(2020–

Divett Chambers, the forerunner of Anthony Mason Chambers, was opened in 1993. It began with the three founding barristers – Tom Birchall, Paul Heywood-Smith and David Wicks – who leased the north half of the building which is divided by an archway. The following year the lease became available for the south side and the chambers then occupied both sides of the building. This created an interesting architectural anomaly of having to go up and down stairs to cross the central arch when moving from one side of the upper level to the other.

The original building was built some time during the 1880s. According to Adelaide City Council archives the Smith Survey of 1880 does not show it. By 1889, it does exist – a warehouse owned by Charles Henry Goode. He was in his sixties by then and had already run a successful "soft–goods" business with his brothers.

Now with a partner in London – Mr W H Durrant – he built up a merchandising business known as Goode Durant & Co., and extended their branches to London, Broken Hill, Perth and Kalgoorlie. Charles Goode was also actively involved in public institutions supporting blind, poor, and invalid people. His legacies in this area are perhaps longest lived: he headed the trust that established Kalyra at Belair, originally for consumptives, and Escourt House at Grange, for crippled children and aged blind people.

In late 2006 Divett Chambers relocated to 201 Victoria Square. Sir Anthony Mason opened the new chambers now named after him. Among his extraordinary list of appointments he was Commonwealth Attorney-General 1964–1969, a justice of the Court of Appeal of NSW 1969–1972 and appointed to the High Court of Australia in 1972. He was Chief Justice 1987–1995, and the 'Mason Court' took the High Court beyond mere legalism. Perhaps its most widely known and influential judgment is Mabo v Queensland (No 2) in 1992, which ended the colonial doctrine of terra nullius.

In October 2006 Vickie Chapman, a member of Anthony Mason Chambers and at the time South Australia's Deputy Leader of the Opposition, mentioned the launch and naming after a High Court chief justice.[1] She wanted to use the occasion to remind her parliamentary colleagues that the Commonwealth government had still never chosen a High Court judge from South Australia.

The building at Victoria Square was once the Marine and Harbour's Department, and located on the corner of Grote Street. In 1979 in order to preserve the historically valuable building it was put on rail tracks and moved to where it is today.

The building narrowly missed being a nightclub. In 2003, the owners of the Planet Hotel sold their hotel and gaming licences to a company with the intention to open a club at 201 Victoria Square. Their landlords, however, claimed that they had the right to those licences for 'NIL' cost, as per the original lease agreement. They took action in 2004. Justice Ann Vanstone agreed with them and that put an end to the plans for the nightclub, thus liberating the building.[2] The licences dispute and its appeals continued their way through the courts until 2018 when the High Court definitively allowed the landlords' appeal.[3] At the time of writing of this book, the dispute over costs continues.

---

1 Hansard, Tuesday 14 November 2006, p. 1205.

2 *Clone Pty Ltd v Players Pty Ltd & Ors* [2005] SASC 281 (22 July 2005)

3 *Clone Pty Ltd v Players Pty Ltd (In Liquidation) (Receivers & Managers Appointed)* [2018] HCA 12 (21 March 2018)

Members of Divett Chambers around 1998: Paul Heywood-Smith, Tom Birchall, David Wicks, Richard Ross-Smith, Paul Slattery. (LSSA)

Sir Anthony Mason launching Anthony Mason Chambers in 2006. Standing to his left are Paul Heywood-Smith, Jo-Anne Deuter and Paul Slattery. (AMC)

Legoe Chambers

Opened: September 1994 at 81 Angas Street; 96 Gouger Street December 2004;
61–63 Carrington Street since 2013

Members in approximate order of joining:

Michael David	(1994–1996) DCSA
Ian Sampson	(1994–1999)
Ann Vanstone	(1994–1999) DCSA
John Ibbotson	(1996–2011)
Michael Barnett	(1996–2011)
David Stokes	(1996–2009)
Ian White	(1998–2013)
Robert Kane	(1998–2013)
Grahame Lang	(2000–2003)
Vasilios Fragos	(2003)
Nicholas Floreani	(2003)
Scott Henchliffe	(2004–2005)
Anne Barnett	(2005–2011)
Matthew Mead	(2009–
Kristie Molloy	(2012–
Carrie Demertzis	(2017–
Rose-Marie Read	(2017–

Christopher Legoe Chambers, now Legoe Chambers, was formed by two Queen's Counsel – Michael David from Bar Chambers and Ann Vanstone from the DPP – and Ian Sampson, a successful lawyer and one–time member of the Police. The chambers were originally situated in Angas Street and from 2004 to 2013 Christopher Legoe Chambers was located in Gouger Street, overlooking China Town. In July 2013, Legoe Chambers moved to its current location at Carrington House.

The Chambers are named after the first barrister to practice at the independent bar in South Australia, The Honourable Christopher Legoe AO QC.

ABOVE: Mr Legoe and Kristie Molloy (Head of Legoe Chambers at publication) at the 2017 SA Bar Dinner. (LC)

Victoria Chambers

3rd Floor, 195 Victoria Square, Adelaide
Opened: February 1996; Closed: 2013

Members in approximate order of joining:

David Greenwell	(1996–2013)
Roger Sallis	(2000–2013)
David Haines	(2005–2013)

David Greenwell co-founded Edmund Barton Chambers, but found himself running out of space. He set himself up again independently as Victoria Chambers and was eventually joined by Roger Sallis. In 2005 another Edmund Barton co-founder, David Haines QC, became the third member.

David Greenwell, David Haines, Roger Sallis. (VC)

Equity Chambers

Level 5, 22 Grenfell Street, Adelaide
Opened: 1997; Closed 2020

Members in approximate order of joining:

Barry Fox	(1997–2002)
Simon Moncrieff	(1997–2002)
Margaret Ross	(1997–2002)
Diana Dibden	(1999–2020)

The barristers at Equity Chambers always maintained a strong independence apart from sharing the name, paying most bills separately and never having shared support staff. Simon Moncrieff moved to Perth, Margaret Ross eventually needed clerical support and moved to Campbell Chambers, and Barry Fox moved to Melbourne. Those three were the founders, but the fourth member who joined later, Di Dibden, remained as the sole member until she retired 30 June 2020.

Howard Zelling Chambers

Level 11, SGIC Building, Adelaide
Opened: 1997; Level 12, 211 Victoria Square, 2013

Members in approximate order of joining:

Neville Rochow	(1997–2013)
(John) Stephen Roder	(1997–2007)
Arturo Dal Cin	(1999–2006)
Michael Magarey	(1999–
Denys Simpson	(1999–2007)
Elisa Holmes	(1999–2001)
Richard Evans	(2002–2007)
Martin Keith	(2001–2013)
Michael Roder	(2003–
Kym Tredrea	(2004–
David Quick	(2004–2008)
Larissa Detmold	(2007–2009)
Graham Edmonds-Wilson	(2007–
Gary Coppola	(2009–2013)
Rachael Gray	(2009–2015)
Ian Colgrave	(2009–
Steven Thomas	(2009–2017)
Alexander Manos	(2012–

Robert Fenwick Elliott	(2013–2014)
Patrick Barry	(2014–
Kirsty Stewart	(2014–
David Billington	(2015–
Stuart Lindsay	(2015–2016)
Debbie De Palma	(2015–
(James) Tom Birchall	(2015–
Damian O'Leary	(2016–2017)
Christina Flourentzou	(2018–2019)
Paul d'Assumpçao	(2019–
Marita Pangallo	(2019–

Neville Rochow had been encouraged by Howard Zelling to join the independent bar in South Australia when Rochow was doing research work for the Law Reform Committee – after first obtaining some experience interstate.

While working in Melbourne on a South Australian case, Peter Eriksen told him that a group was setting up new chambers in Franklin Street – Paul Cuthbertson, David Greenwell, David Haines and Sydney Tilmouth. Neville Rochow returned to Adelaide and joined them and remained with what evolved evolved into Edmund Barton Chambers on Wright Street.

That was around 1987 and Rochow stayed with Edmund Barton until 1992. He found that chambers in bluestone buildings had the downside of cramped quarters and he needed more space. He moved to 14 Flinders Street for three years shared facilities with Steve Roder.

When space became available in the SGIC building in January 1997, the pair took it. In 1999 more space became available on the 11th floor and the set of chambers undertook the first of what would be several expansions, naming the new, larger grouping Howard Zelling Chambers. One incidental advantage in this location was a spectacular view, something that Neville

Rochow had cherished during his time with Baker and McKenzie in a high-rise office in Melbourne.

Howard Zelling Chambers around 2000. Standing: Martin Keith, Arturo Dal Cin, Steve Roder, Michael Magarey, Denys Simpson. Seated: Elisa Holmes, Neville Rochow. (HZC)

Room with a view: Steve Roder with an 11th floor view. (HZC)

Liz Mammone (then Clerk of Chambers), Elisa Holmes, Steve Roder, Neville Rochow. (HZC)

Howard Zelling Chambers reception in 2020. Liz Mammone (then Clerk of Chambers) with Steve Roder. (HZC)

Sir Mellis Napier Chambers

18–20 Grenfell Street, Adelaide (North)
201 Victoria Square, Adelaide (South)
Open 2000–2003

Members in approximate order of joining:

Andrew Jordan	(2000–2003)
Stuart Lindsay	(2000–2003)
Vickie Chapman	(2000–2003)
Meredith Dickson	(2001–2003)
Kevin Borick	(2002–2003)
(Eleanor) Frances Nelson	(2002–2003)
David Whittle	(2001–2003)

Wright Chambers

66 Wright Street, Adelaide
Opened: 1 July 2001; from 2006 at Level 2, 366 King William Street as Wright Chambers, closed 2020[1]

Members in approximate order of joining:

Mark Griffin	(1997–2009) DCSA
Margaret Kelly	(1998–2017) DCSA
Elizabeth Shepphard	(1998–)
Heather Mack	(1998–)
Paul Tothill	(1998–)
Barry Amey	(2000–)
John Firth	(2000–)
(Frank) Christopher Brohier	(2001–2006)
Stuart Cole	(2001–)
Stephen McEwen	(2001–)

Wright Street Chambers in 2001 was formed by barristers who were already practising individually at the same premises for up to four years. The first was Mark Griffin, who moved into 66 Wright Street in 1997 to practise as an independent barrister after returning from the United States where he had worked as a Public Defender.

Over the next few years the number of independently practising barristers grew. More office space became available on the ground floor and it became obvious that with the arrival of Christopher Brohier, Stuart Cole and Stephen McEwen that advantages could be gained by pooling resources. Thus the ten barristers listed above are the founding members.

1 Details were not available at time of publication.

The set of chambers differs from many of the older sets such as Bar and Jeffcott in that it does not seek to emulate English chambers. In Wright Street there are no mahogany desks with leather inserts surrounded by wall–to–ceiling bookshelves groaning under the weight of law reports dating back decades. But nevertheless, the naming of the chambers from the address it

Members of Wright Street Chambers published in the LSSA Bulletin October 2001 issue. Back row: Stephen McEwen, Christopher Brohier, John Firth, Pat Amey. Middle Row: Elizabeth Sheppard, Mark Griffin, Antonietta Tavella (clerk), Margaret Kelly. Front Row: Josie Malatesta (clerk) Paul Tothill, Heather Mack, Stuart Cole. (LSSA)

Elizabeth Evatt Chambers

Level 1, 51 Angas Street, Adelaide
Opened: 2004

Members in approximate order of joining:

Meredith Dickson	(2004–
Taanya Lewis	(2004–
David Childs	(2004–2014)
Nicholas Eid	(2008–2014)
Jane Miller	(2019–
Mark Anderson	(2020–

Meredith Dickson and Taanya Lewis established a specialist family law chambers in 2004. They named it in honour of Australia's first Chief Justice of the Family Court of Australia, setting a strong association to its practice and values.

Among her achievements, Elizabeth Evatt AC (born 1933) was the first female Australian federal judge and the first Australian elected to the United Nations Human Rights Committee. As a student she had won the University of Sydney's medal for law in 1955, and a scholarship to Harvard where she earned an LLM in 1956 and then was admitted to Inner Temple in London.

After her return to Australia she chaired the Royal Commission on Human Relationships, which led to the Family Law Act 1975 both establishing no-fault divorce and the Family Court of Australia. Just some of her appointments include Deputy President of the Commonwealth Conciliation and Arbitration Commission from 1974 to 1989, a member of the United Nations Committee on the Elimination of Discrimination Against Women from 1984 to 1992, chairing it for two years; a Commissioner of the Australian Human Rights and Equal Opportunity Commission from 1995 to 1998, a judge on the World Bank Tribunal from 1998 to 2007 and a Commissioner of the International Committee of Jurists in 2003.

Christopher Legoe (right) launches Elizabeth Evatt Chambers in 2004. L-R Founders Taanya Lewis, Meredith Dickson. (EEC)

Elliott Johnston Chambers

356A King Williams Street
Opened: 14 October 2004

Members in approximate order of joining:

Nicholas (Nick) Niarchos	(2004–2013)
Paul Rofe	(2004–2013)
Steven Churches	(2005–
Robert Sallis	(2005–2009)
Greg Stevens	(2005–
Helen Pertsinidis	(2010)
Angus J Redford	(2009–
John Dillon	(2011–
Rosie Read	(2011–2016
Ian Roberts	(2013–2017
David Fabbro	(2014–
Philip Saunders	(2016–
Adrian Maik	(2017–
Grant Algie	(2017–
Jane Powell	(2017–
Alex Panousakis	(2017–
Elizabeth Mansfield	(2018–

In 2004, Nick Niarchos AM approached colleague, Paul Rofe QC to establish a new set of barristers' chambers in Adelaide.

Nick Niarchos, Elliott Johnston, Paul Rofe and portrait painter Sophie Downey. (EJC)

Back Row: John Dillon, Steven Churches, Angus Redford, Grant Algie, Adrian Maik. Front row: David Fabbro, Alex Panousakis, Jane Powell, Elizabeth Mansfield, Greg Stevens. (EJC)

Paul John Lawrence Rofe QC (1948–2013) was a prominent South Australian criminal barrister and the former South Australian Director of Public Prosecutions, a position he held from 1992 to 2004. Paul was admitted to practice in 1973 and appointed a Queen's Counsel in 1991.

Nicholas Niarchos was highly respected litigation lawyer who often represented the "impecunious underdog". Nick was made a Member of the Order of Australia in the 1999 Queen's Birthday Honours List for service to the Greek community of South Australia through groups providing social welfare, cultural, education and sporting programmes.

Elliott Johnston (1918–2011) was admitted as a legal practitioner in 1940 and after war service he entered legal practice. A passionate advocate, Elliott appeared for everyone, often representing the underdog, usually a worker. Indeed, he was a friend of the oppressed all his life.

Elliott Johnston was appointed Queen's Counsel in 1970 following a political controversy associated with his prior membership of the Communist Party of Australia. Elliott was a highly regarded silk and was appointed as a Justice of the Supreme Court of South Australia where he served (1983–1988) with legal distinction, compassion, and wisdom. He was later appointed by the Federal Government as the second Royal Commissioner into Aboriginal Deaths in Custody (1989–1991).

After retirement Elliott maintained an active involvement with the law for some years through his role as Editor of the South Australian State Reports, as a commentator and as an Associate Professor at Flinders University Law School. He was co–patron, with Dr Lowitja O'Donohue, of Reconciliation SA.

A more detailed exposition of Elliott's biography and achievements is contained in the book Red Silk: The Life of Elliott Johnston QC by Penelope Debelle.

A prominent human rights advocate Nick Niarchos AM recalls the day he approached the ever–modest Elliott Johnston seeking his permission for their Chambers to honour him. Mr Johnston was kind enough to agree but expressed surprise, saying he thought "you'd need to be well and truly gone before they'd name a Chambers after you."

Nick and Paul operated their new Chambers in modest offices above the Police Union Club in Carrington Street Adelaide. To accommodate Elliott Johnson Chambers' growing numbers, in July 2005 it moved to 356A King William Street.

(text courtesy of Greg Stevens, EJC)

Hugh Burton Chambers

Level 4/22 Grenfell Street; 3/366 King William Street
Opened: 2004

Members in approximate order of joining:

Joseph Bowler	(2004–2018)
Vickianne West	(2004–2020)
Holly Tinning (née Leeson)	(2004–
John McGinn	(2006–
Judith Cocks	(2008–
Melissa Boyle (née Perry)	(2019–

Vickianne West and Louise Bedson commenced South Australia's first all female barristers chambers at Dover Chambers, Dover House, Kensington Road, Kensington Gardens in 1997, specialising in Family Law and Costs.

When Louise Bedson moved to Sydney in 2003, Vickianne West left Dover Chambers to found Hugh Burton Chambers with Joseph Bowler and Holly Tinning (née Leeson) at the Executive Trustee building, 22 Grenfell Street Adelaide. The Chambers was named with the permission of the late Hugh Burton, a retired Judge of the Family Court of Australia based in Adelaide from 1986 to 1999.

Upon the Family Court of Australia relocating its Adelaide Registry to Angas Street the Chambers moved to 3/366 King William Street Adelaide and expanded when Mr John McGinn joined in 2006. In 2008 Miss Judith Cocks joined the chambers which then specialised exclusively in Family Law.

In 2018 Mr Bowler left Chambers to practice on his own accord and Ms Melissa Boyle (née Perry) joined the Chambers in 2019.

Vickianne West ceased practising as a barrister in 2020 but continues to practice as a mediator based at the Chambers.

Today the members of Hugh Burton Chambers continue to specialise in Family Law. The present Clerks are Ms Daniela Pollina and Mrs Sandy Davis.

The entry to Hugh Burton Chambers in King William Street with the photograph of Hugh Burton.

Len King Chambers

Opened: 2010 at level 6, 185 Victoria Square

Members in approximate order of joining:

Heath Barklay	(2010–2014)
Kristopher Handshin	(2010--2014)
Peter Morrison	(2012–2019)
Anthony Allen	(2012–
Jane Abbey	(2012–
Liesl Chapman	(2012–2017) DCSA
Michelle Barnes	(2013–
Ian White	(2013–2015) AMC
Edward Jolly	(2013–
William Boucaut	(2015–
Andrew Culshaw	(2015–
Andrew Fowler-Walker	(2015–2020)
Christopher Allen	(2018–
James Marcus	(2019–
Samuel McDonough	(2020–
Emily Telfer	(2020–

The Hon. Leonard (Len) James King AC QC (1925–2011) was the real force behind the first five years of Don Dunstan's 1970s decade as Premier. Len King was Attorney-General from 1970 to 1975, and introduced a series of social reforms that resonate to the present: consumer protection, social welfare and community support, and abolition of corporal and capital punishment. He set the long and continuing path to the erasure of sexual and racial discrimination. South Australia under Don Dunstan and Len King led Australia's social reforms.

He was appointed to the Supreme Court in 1975 and was Chief Justice from 1978 until 1995. In that time he significantly strenghtened the independence of the judiciary with the establishment of the Courts Administration Authority.

L-R Christopher Allen, Samuel McDonough, Michelle Barnes, Andrew Culshaw, Anthony Allen, Edward Jolly, James Marcus, Jane Abbey, Bill Boucaut. (LCC)

Victoria Square Chambers

Level 2, 195 Victoria Square, Adelaide
Opened: 2015

Members in approximate order of joining:

Rachael Gray	(2015–
Natalie Charlesworth	(2015–2016) FCA
Paris Dean	(2019–

Dr Rachael Gray co-founded Victoria Square Chambers in 2015 with Natalie Charlesworth, who was appointed to the Federal Court of Australia to replace John Mansfield, to whom she had early in her career been a Judge's Associate. In 2019 Paris Dean joined chambers after returning from interstate.

Chambers entrance 2020. (courtesy Rachael Gray)

Selby Street Chambers

28 Selby Street, Adelaide
Opened: July 2017

Members in approximate order of joining:

Andrew Collett	(2017–
Simon Blewett	(2017–
Dan O'Gorman	(2017–
Ron Levy	(2017–
Anne Sibree	(2019–

Selby Street Chambers formed in 2017 with four barristers seeking to build a group focusing on Aboriginal, industrial, employment, human rights, anti-discrimination, administrative and personal injury cases. Three of their founding members have practised interstate and the chambers and all members are associate members of Roma Mitchell Chambers in Brisbane.

Nexus Chambers

Level 3, 19 Gouger Street, Adelaide
Opened: October 2020

Members in approximate order of joining:

Darren Blight	(2020–
Scott Evans	(2020–
Edward (Ted) Guthrie	(2020–
David Blyth	(2020–
Lewis Gentry	(2020–
William (Will) Mellor	(2020–
Michael Tilley	(2020–
Thomas Rice	(2020–

Nexus Chambers was founded by Darren Blight QC and Scott Evans in mid 2020. Soon thereafter, an additional four founding members joined, namely, Ted Guthrie, Lewis Gentry, David Blyth and William Mellor. Nexus Chambers arose out of a vision to break the mould of the traditional style and operation of barristers' chambers in Adelaide towards a more flexible and adaptable chambers model. For example, smaller rooms would be planned for barristers starting out to lower the initial financial outlay, and larger rooms for those who are longer established.

Based at 19 Gouger Street, Adelaide in a new, contemporary office space with bespoke fit-out and technology, Nexus Chambers also has the unique distinction of being the only barristers' chambers in Adelaide to be located immediately next to the Supreme Court of South Australia.

Nexus Chambers founding members prior to works beginning on level 3, 19 Gouger Street: Darren Blight, Ted Guthrie, Scott Evans, David Blyth, William Mellor and Lewis Gentry. (NC)

Part Three

Silks

Chapter Four

Queen's and Senior Counsel Appointments 1974–2020

This chapter lists all the Queen's Counsel appointments made between 1974 and May 2008, then Senior Counsel appointments from then until October 2020, organised in approximate order of appointment. The list updates Graham Loughlin's in his History Honours thesis completed in 1974. This thesis is available in the Law School Library of the University of Adelaide and is an invaluable reference in tracing South Australia's senior legal practitioners of its period.

The list of Queen's and Senior Counsel here maintains Graham Loughlin's format and varies only in that this one is more oriented to the independent bar. Thus we list the date that the Queen's and Senior Counsel signed the bar roll and what set or sets of chambers – if any – they worked from. Other activities, if they are numerous, are selected according to their relevance to a career at the independent bar. As a result, in some cases there will be more information available in *Who's Who* listings as these cover the whole of a person's life.

Complete records of Queen's and Senior Counsel appointments are not kept in any of the Government offices: Government House, Attorney-General's Office, Chief Justice's Chambers – nor by the Law Society or Bar Association. Loughlin's list and this one together therefore make up the only complete record.

Names are listed with their QC or SC, and as diligently as possible, any government post-nominal letters. Titles from judicial appointments past or present are not listed.

Graham Loughlin catalogued 76 appointments, beginning with the first three in 1865, over a period of 109 years. The legal profession over this time grew from around 70 to approximately 500. In the 45 years since there have been 115 appointments and the profession has grown in size to 3,500 practitioners. As of late 2020 there were approximately 35 practising Queen's Counsel. This is around a seventh of the independent bar.

Much has changed since 1974. Loughlin could only list one female among his 76 – Roma Mitchell in 1962. The next female appointment was Frances Nelson in 1982, who is the first female member of the independent bar to achieve that distinction. There have now been a total of 19 females appointed including Roma Mitchell of the total 191 since 1865.

A major professional difference in this group was the 1979 ruling by Chief Justice Len King that appointees to silk from that date must join the independent bar. Once they signed the bar roll, this then also tied them to the rules governing practice as an independent barrister. Prior to this, the expectation that silks would keep out of the Magistrate's and Industrial Courts and not do menial solicitor's work was informal, although generally heeded.

Appointments to silk were originally made on the recommendation of the Chief Justice, but until 2008 the government had the prerogative to accept them. There were nine cases between 1865 and 2008 where the government of the day questioned recommendations. Six of these were delayed – J R Anderson and A W Piper (1908), W J Isbister and H A Parsons (1914), E F Johnston (1969) and J D Edwardson – and three never appointed – H E Downer (1890), J Russell (1900) and A Buchanan (1900).

Until 2008 the government of South Australia also had the power in theory to make their own appointments to Queen's Counsel. This appears to have been used only the once. In 1965, Attorney-General Don Dunstan appointed himself as he believed the title would enhance the standing of that office.

In April 1960, of the four appointments made by Sir Mellis Napier, one was his son Robert, who the profession did not consider of the appropriate qualifications. The Law Society of South Australia's Council on 26 April 1960 decided that appointments should be from then on initiated by applications from candidates themselves, and that the Law Society should be consulted by the Chief Justice on its view of candidates' suitability. As it would turn out, Robert had his appointment revoked in 1971.

Sir Mellis Napier was reluctant to accept applications and the Law Society Council revoked this measure at a meeting that same year on 29 October. Further attempts to introduce candidate-initiated appointments had to wait for the appointment of John Bray in 1967. In August that year, the Law Society Council with the agreement of John Bray introduced the system that practitioners seeking silk notify the Chief Justice by September each year.

The controversy that erupted over the appointment of Elliott Johnston in November 1969 is probably unique, and it was a good test of what the appointment meant at that point. Was Queen's Counsel a purely professional appointment, made only according to the applicant's professional ability and standing? Or was it still to be taken at its literal, traditional role as conferred originally by Elizabeth I on Sir Francis Bacon in 1596? According to two University of Adelaide Law School lecturers in 1970, W B Fisse and D St Leger Kelly who published an article in the *Australian Law Journal* on the matter in July 1970, the answer by this time was on professional ability only:

> The problems which had been encountered stemmed largely from the failure of the Regulations in South Australia (and elsewhere) to mirror the changed status and position of Queen's Counsel. Although as we have seen earlier, Queen's Counsel were originally advocates employed by the Crown, their position had changed so radically since the mid–eighteenth century that the title itself had become a misleading one. At least since the abolition in 1921 of the requirement of a licence to appear against the Crown, the rank of Queen's Counsel could only properly be regarded as a professional, and in no sense a governmental, position.[1]

One sign that the title "Queen's Counsel" designated its holder as a Counsel to the monarch would have been the annuity of forty pounds that was first granted to Francis Bacon in 1604 by James I to retain him as his "King's Learned Counsel". But as William Holdsworth shows in his short article in 1920, "The Rise of the Order of King's Counsel", these annuities did not last much longer than James I's reign. By the end of the seventeenth century, this new order of counsel was "already ceasing to be in any real sense the king's counsel, chosen more 'out of favour than merit' in the profession".

Then, as Fisse and St Leger Kelly tell us, the licence required to appear against the Crown has not been necessary since 1921, at least in South Australia. The licence was the last vestige of any suggestion of formal service to the Crown. Since then, the title of "Queen's Counsel" has been only a designation of ability, that the title holder is sufficiently skilled to lead complex litigation.

The change to "Senior Counsel"

New South Wales was the first Australian State to introduce the title of "Senior Counsel", in 1993, followed by Queensland in 1994, ACT in 1995, Victoria in 2000, Western Australia in 2001, Tasmania in 2005, and in 2007 the Northern Territory amended its Supreme Court rules to allow additionally the title of "Senior Counsel". In 2007 New Zealand also introduced Senior Counsel.

As early as 2004 the Labor Party Attorney-General Michael Atkinson had signalled that "the recognition of South Australia's leading barristers may change in the future after a resolution of ALP State Convention last weekend." South Australia became the last Australian State to introduce the title, on 12 May 2008.

With the new letters across the country a first concern emerged. The letters "SC" are not patented like those of "QC", so nothing prevented law firms adding "SC" to selected senior partners to designate them as "Special Counsel". In their defence, solicitors have never had access to an official senior post-nominal. In 2020 Attorney-General Vickie Chapman estimated that there were up to 200 "Special Counsel"s around South Australia's law firms.

Another concern was that regional Commonwealth jurisdictions such as Hong Kong, Malaysia and Singapore, who had also ended the title of "Queen's Counsel", were for whatever reason showing a preference to hiring Queen's Counsel for complex litigation, even from as far as England.

Across the Tasman Sea, New Zealand Attorney-General Christopher Finlayson commented in June 2009, just two years after introducing Senior Counsel:

> The government has responded to concerns from the legal profession and will restore the title of Queen's Counsel to recognise outstanding members of the independent bar. The title Queen's Counsel is instantly recognised as providing a certain standard of legal advice both among the New Zealand public and internationally.

In December 2012, Queensland's Attorney-General commented on that trend in a speech committing to the reintroduction of the older title:

> The feedback I have received raised concerns that SC was often mistaken for the term Special Counsel, which many law firms have taken to using for solicitors. QC

> is also more widely known and understood by the public as a mark of professional distinction at the Bar and this move will make the distinction much clearer. It is important that Queensland silks are competitive internationally particularly in Singapore and Hong Kong where the use of QCs is preferred. Asian countries employ QCs from as far as the United Kingdom and this change will give Queensland leverage over other Australian states competing for a share of this market.

New Zealand reinstated Queen's Counsel in November 2012 and Queensland in 2013. Of the 74 Queensland Senior Counsel appointed in the intervening 18 years, 70 elected for the change to Queen's Counsel. New appointments in both New Zealand and Queensland are Queen's Counsel.

In 2014, Victoria reintroduced Queen's Counsel, but this time as an option for appointees who as before were first appointed Senior Counsel. This was the first time that a jurisdiction offered a choice of title. This was a model that appealed to the South Australian bar.

On 17 March 2018 South Australia found itself with a Liberal government for the first time in around 16 years. The South Australian Bar Association passed a motion at its annual general meeting on 1 August 2018 expressing strong support for the option of the title of Queen's Counsel, along the lines of the Victorian model.

Around that time the Law Society of South Australia circulated a survey to its 3,444 members. Almost a quarter responded, a record 843. Of those, 67% agreed to there being a choice.

Strong support for the choice model across the profession convinced South Australian Attorney-General Vickie Chapman to offer it. All applications for silk would still be for the title of Senior Counsel, but once appointed, those who wished to be known as Queen's Counsel could apply to the Attorney-General and swap.

However, in 2008 when Chief Justice John Doyle and the Rann Labor government replaced the title of Queen's Counsel with Senior Counsel, the Supreme Court also gained sole prerogative for their appointment. The Court saw that arrangement as strengthening the independence of the judiciary and the profession.

Chief Justice Chris Kourakis viewed the plan between the Attorney-General and the South Australian Bar Association as a potential abrogation of the Supreme Court's hard-won exclusive power over the appointment process. After the Senior Counsel appointments made in October 2018, he put further appointments on hold.

In January 2019, the Bar Association's President, Mark Hoffmann QC, confirmed that the Association did not want any change to the current appointment process, nor to give Executive government any prerogative role in appointments: "The model proposed by the SA Bar that is before the Government for consideration mirrors and adopts that in place in Victoria. It has operated in Victoria with a Labor Government in place without any difficulty."

In early 2019 the Attorney-General offered all the existing 39 Senior Counsel the option to change to Queen's Counsel. Of the 39 Senior Counsel, 17 took the option and their title changes were gazetted officially on 26 April 2019.

The Legal Practitioners (Senior and Queen's Counsel) Amendment Bill began its path through Parliament. In July 2020 the Chief Justice acknowledged that it addressed the primary concerns of the judges to protect the independence of the judiciary. The Supreme Court retained its power over all appointments to Senior Counsel, with only persons so appointed able to request a titular change to Queen's Counsel. The Bill empowered the Court to revoke appointments of Senior and Queen's Counsel. The South Australian Bar Association also was happy the Bill settled their concerns. It finally passed in September 2020. When the first appointees are made they will be the first ones in all South Australia's history to have an immediate choice of title.

Horton (Tim) Clement Williams QC

photo courtesy LSSA

son of: H R Williams
born: 21 April 1933

educated: Newington College (Sydney), University of Adelaide (LLB)
articles with: Piper Bakewell and Piper
admitted: 1955
QC 1974

career: Judge's Associate 1954–1956; joined independent bar 1977; President SA Bar Association 1984–1986; Chairman Legal Practitioners Discipline Tribunal 1989–1995; Chairman Gaming Supervisory Authority 1995; Dep. Chairman Judicial Conference Australia 2000–2002
Justice Supreme Court SA 1995–2003

married: 1958 Helen (dec. 1991) 1s 1d; 1996 Marie

Clubs: Royal South Australian Yacht Squadron (Commander 1991–1993)

Derek Willoughby Bollen QC

photo courtesy LSSA

son of: K W Bollen
born: 1 April 1927 died 9 January 2007

educated: St Peters College, University of Adelaide (LLB)
articles with: J F Astley, 1947–1950
admitted: 18 December 1950
QC 1974

career: joined independent bar 1974; member Hanson Chambers 1977–1982; President Law Society SA 1980–1982; Jnr Vice-President Law Council Australia 1980–1982; Law Reform Committee SA 1975–1982; publication: *Motor Vehicle Law* 1983
Justice Supreme Court of South Australia 1982–1997

married: 1955 Anne (dec. 1974) 2s 1d (2) 1976 Marina Kirsch Clubs: Adelaide, Royal Adelaide Golf
Recreation: golf, tennis, bridge, cricket, music

John William von Doussa AO QC

photo courtesy HREOC website

son of: F W L von Doussa solicitor and M L von Doussa
born: 17 September 1940

educated: St Peters College, University of Adelaide (LLB)
articles with: Thomson Hogarth Ross & Lewis 1961–1962; admitted: 1963
QC 1978

career: joined independent bar 1978, member Bar Chambers 1978–1981; Jeffcott Chambers 1982–1987; Tutor University of Adelaide Law of Procedure 1965–1968; Special Investigator Elder Smith takeover 1982–1983; President Law Society SA 1982–1983; Justice Supreme Court of South Australia 1986–1988, Justice Federal Court of Australia 1988–2003; Australian Law Reform Commission since 1992; Judge Industrial Relations Court of Australia since 1994, President Australian Competition Tribunal since 1999, Judge Court of Appeal Vanuatu since 1997, Judge Supreme Court of Fiji since 2003, President Human Rights and Equal Opportunities Commission 2003–2008; Chancellor University of Adelaide 2004–2010; Doctor of the University of Adelaide 2011.

married: 1964 Joanna 4s 1d (dec. 1993), 1997 Julie 1s 1d

Kenneth Ramsay McCarthy QC

photo courtesy LSSA

son of: James Crimean Ellery McCarthy (solicitor) and Gwendolin Helen née Ure (Stow Scholar, solicitor)
born: 25 October 1935, died 3 May 1998

educated: Kadina High School, Rostrevor College, University of Adelaide (LLB) articles with: Arthur Pickering 1956–57 (Pickering, Cornish & Lempriere Abbott
admitted: 10 February 1958
QC 1978

career: Tutor in Workers' Compensation, University of Adelaide; Minda Home Board, Chairman Glenside Hospital Board, Chairman Psychology Board, Wing Commander – Judge Advocate Legal Corps RAAF

married: 1960 Janine née Fitzgerald
Clubs: Grange Golf Club, Naval and Military Club.

Edward Picton Mullighan QC

photo courtesy LSSA

son of: Frederick Edward Mullighan (electrician) and Emily Picton Mullighan (musician)
born: 25 March 1939, died 16 September 2011

educated: Pulteney Grammar, University of Adelaide (final certificate)
articles with: R R St C Chamberlain QC 1958–1959 (Crown Solicitor), J R Kearnan QC (Crown Solicitor) 1959–1961; admitted: 1962
QC 1978

career: Associate to Mr Justice Brazel 1961, Associate to Sir Roderick Chamberlain 1961–1962, President LSSA 1978–1980, Chairman LSSA Advocacy Group & Instructor in Advocacy, joined independent bar 1983, member Jeffcott Chambers 1983–1988, Royal Commissions as Counsel Assisting: Moratorium Demonstrations (1971–1972), Dismissal of a School Student, Dismissal of the Police Commissioner (1978), Monarto Transactions; Co–Chair Reconciliation South Australia, Chairman Aboriginal Cultural Awareness Programme for the Judiciary, Chairman Restorative Justice Centre; Justice Supreme Ct SA 1989–2005
Commissioner, Children In State Care: Commission Of Inquiry Allegations Of Sexual Abuse And Death From Criminal Conduct 2005–2008.

married: 1963 Jan

Graham Clifton Prior QC

photo courtesy LSSA

son of: H S Prior
born: 2 April 1938 died 2014

educated: Unley High, University of Adelaide (LLB), Oxford University (BCL) articles with: J F Astley QC 1960
admitted: 1960
QC 1978

career: Judge's Associate to Sir Mellis Napier and Sir Bruce Ross, tutor and lecturer in law University of Adelaide 1964–1970, Crown Solicitor SA 1976–1984, Chairman Adelaide Festival of Arts 1984–1988, Chairman State Opera Co. SA 1982–1985, Chairman Electoral Districts Boundaries Commission 2002 Justice Supreme Court SA 1984–2004.

married: 1961 Anne 2d Recreation: films, music, art, travel

Kevin Patrick Duggan QC

photo courtesy LSSA

son of: P L Duggan
born: 25 July 1941

educated: Rostrevor College, University of Adelaide articles with: Alderman Clark Ligertwood & Price
admitted: 1965
QC 1979

career: Judge's Associate to Sir Edward McTiernan (High Court) 1965–1966, joined independent bar 1980, member Bar Chambers 1980–1988, Lecturer in Criminal Procedure 1971–1987, Crown Prosecutor 1971–1979, President SA Bar Association 1986–1988, Judge Advocate-General ADF 1996–2001
Justice Supreme Court SA 1988–2011, AM 2002

married: 1969 Rosemary 3s 1d Clubs: Adelaide, Naval, Military and Air Force

Robin Rhodes Millhouse QC

photo courtesy LSSA

son of: Vivian Rhodes Millhouse (Justice Supreme Ct SA 1961–1963) and Grace Lilly Ayliffe
born: 9 December 1929 died 28 April 2017

educated: St Peters College, St Marks College, University of Adelaide (LLB)
articles with: Vivian Millhouse, Baker, McEwin, Millhouse & Ligertwood, 1948 to 1951 admitted: 1951
QC 1979

career: joined independent bar 1964 (founding member), member Bar Chambers 1965–1982, MP Mitcham SA 1955–1982, Attorney-General SA 1968–1970, State Leader New Liberal Movement 1976–1977, State Leader Australian Democrats 1977–1982, Justice Supreme Ct SA 1982–1999, Chief Justice High Ct Kiribati 2000–2011

married: 1957 Margaret (dec. 1992) 3d 2s Clubs: Naval and Military, Adelaide, Harriers Athletic (Adelaide), The Lagoon (Ambo Sth Tarawa), Royal Automobile Club Australia (Sydney)
Recreation: triathlon, long distance running, bike riding, swimming, nude sun–bathing

John William Perry AO QC

photo courtesy *Advertiser*/John Perry

son of: Yannis Gabriel Pieris (born in Farmagusta, Cyprus) and Mildred Harwood (Liverpool, UK)
born: 2 June 1937 died 7 May 2007

educated: Adelaide Boys High, University of Adelaide (LLB) articles with: Michael White admitted: 1960 QC 1979

career: joined independent bar 1980, Head Bar Chambers 1980–1988, Chairman SA Commonwealth Committee Discrimination Employment and Occupation 1976–1978, Faculty of Law University of Adelaide 1984–1998, Bd Examiners Supreme Ct SA 1979–1988, President Law Society SA 1984–1985, Founding Chair, John Bray Law Chapter, University of Adelaide Alumni Association 1993–1995, Council University of. Adelaide 1995–2007 Justice Supreme Court of SA 1988–2007

married: 1958 Jennifer 2s 1d
Clubs: Adelaide Musical: Elder Conservatorium 1951–1957, SA Symphony Orchestra 1955–1957, Leader Burnside Orchestra 1959–1962

Anthony Vincent Russell QC

photo courtesy LSSA

son of: V Russell (solicitor) born: 7 July 1929

educated: Denstone College (Staffordshire), University of Adelaide (LLB) articles with: Baker McEwin (James Robinson and Gordon Bleby) 1964–1967 admitted: 1967 QC 1979

career: joined independent bar 1971, LSSA Council, Judge Industrial Court SA 1980–1994, Judge District Court SA 1989–1999, Judge Environment, Resources and Development Court 1996–1999

married: 1957 Nancy 2s 1d Clubs: Naval Military and Airforce Of interest: Was a purser for P & O 1950–1958; Chevalier of the Sovereign Order of St John of Jerusalem (Knights Hospitaller) (KSJ) 1996, Knight Commander of Grace of the Sovereign Order of St John of Jerusalem (Knights Hospitallers) (KCSJ) 2002

David Norman Angel QC

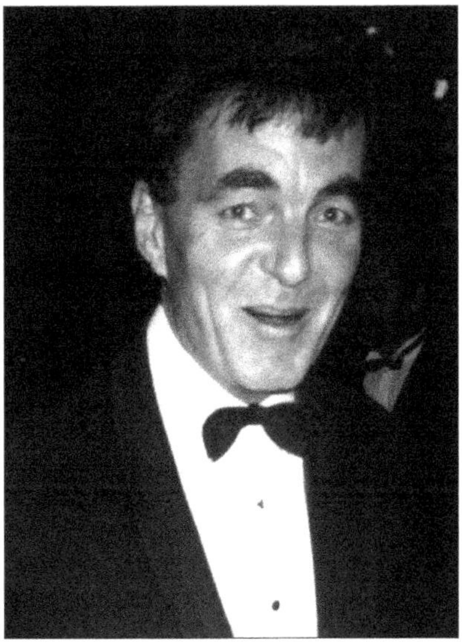

photo courtesy LSSA

son of: Norman Sidney Angel and Muriel Arnold Angel
born: 5 July 1944

educated: Prince Alfred College, University of Adelaide (LLB) articles with: Don Brebner, Fisher Jeffries Taylor and Brebner 1966–1967 admitted: 1967
QC 1981

career: joined Independent bar 1975, Member Bar Chambers 1975–1989, President SA Bar Association 1988–1989, Chairman SA Parole Board 1982–1984, Justice Supreme Court of Northern Territory 1989–2010

married: 1966 (1) 1993 (2) Clubs: Adelaide Recreation: tennis, art galleries, music, reading

John Jeremy Doyle AC QC

photo courtesy John Doyle

son of: J M Doyle Railway Officer and M M Doyle Home Duties
born: 4 April 1945

educated: St Ignatius College, University of Adelaide (LLB Hons 1966), Oxford University (BCL 1967)
articles with: J M White 1966–1967; 1970, J W Perry 1970
admitted: 1970
QC 1981

career: Tutor and lecturer University of Adelaide 1971–1982, joined Independent bar 1977, founding member Hanson Chambers 1977–1985; Chairman Legal Services Commission SA 1985–1986; President SA Bar Association 1989–1990, 1993–1995; Pro–Chancellor Flinders University 1988–2001; Chairman National Judicial College of Australia from its establishment in 2002 to 30 June 2007; Companion of the Order of Australia 2002;
Honorary Doctor of Laws Flinders University 2002
Honorary Doctorate University of Adelaide 2008
Solicitor–General SA 1986–1995
Chief Justice Supreme Court SA 1995–2012

married: 1969 Marie 3d 2s

Eleanor Frances Nelson QC

photo courtesy LSSA

daughter of: R Nelson (Industrial chemist) and E M Nelson (teacher) born: 7 May 1944
educated: Adelaide Girls High, University of Adelaide (LLB)
articles with: P N Waye; admitted: 1967
QC 1982

career: joined independent bar 1984, (founding) member Rose Park Chambers 1982–1990; 1997–2002, John Bray Chambers 1990–1997, Sir Mellis Napier Chambers 2002–2003, Napier Chambers 2004, Bd Examiners Supreme Ct 1975–1989, Law Society Council 1976–1982, Chairman Parole Board SA since 1983, Chairman Casino Supervising Authority 1990–1995

married: 1972 Earle 1s 1d Clubs: Oakbank Hunt, Master SA Jockey, Oakbank Racing

David John Bleby QC

photo courtesy David Bleby

son of: Rev. Canon John Raymond and Mary Kingsnorth Bleby
born: 10 June 1941

educated: St Peters College, University of Adelaide (LLB) Australian College of Theology (ThA) articles with: G E H Bleby Baker McEwin & Co admitted: 1964
QC 1982

career: joined independent bar 1982, member Jeffcott Chambers 1982–1997; Litigation Committee Law Council of Australia 1996–1997; Law Curriculum Committee Law Faculty University of Adelaide 1982–1997, SA Law Reform Inst since 2011, Adjunct Prof Law University of Adelaide since 2011; publications: (contributor) Halsbury's Laws of Australia 1993–2002; Review and Report, The Hon. The Attorney-General: Industrial Relations Court and Commission (SA) 2013; South Australian Civil and Administrative Tribunal: Statutory Review and Report 2017
Justice Supreme Court SA 1997–2012

Chancellor Anglican Diocese of Adelaide 1995–2016, Appellate Tribunal Anglican Church of Australia 1995–2010, Chair of Committees General Synod Anglican Church of Australia 1992–2010, President, Professional Standards Board, Diocese of Adelaide since 2016
Primatial Chancellor, Anglican Church of Australia since 2020

Public Interest Advocate, Telecommunications (Interception and Access) Act 1979 (C'th) since 2016
Parole Administrative Review Commissioner since 2016

married: Elizabeth Mary Abbie 1966
2s 1d Clubs: Adelaide recreation: bellringing, natural heritage conservation, classical and choral music, theatre, wine, golf

Bruce Malcolm Debelle AO QC

photo courtesy LSSA

son of: G A W Debelle
born: 25 June 1938

educated: St Peters College, St Marks College, University of Adelaide (LLB) articles with: Robert Mohr 1959–1960, Samuel J Jacobs 1962
admitted: 1962
QC 1982

career: Tennyson Medal 1956, Associate to Justice Sir Victor Windeyer High Court of Australia 1961–1962, joined independent bar 1983, member Bar Chambers 1983–1990, Australian Law Reform Commission 1978–1984, Vice-President Law Society SA 1989–1990, Executive Law Council of Australia 1987–1990, Chairman Australian String Quartet since 1998, Councillor Walkerville 1970–1977, Lecturer and Tutor, University of Adelaide 1963–1973
Justice Supreme Court of SA 1990–2008
AO 2010

married: 1965 Barbara (dec. 1984) 1s 1d (2) 1986 Pamela Nash Clubs: Adelaide, Mt Lofty Golf Recreation: swimming, music, reading, farming

Malcolm Forgan Gray QC

photo courtesy LSSA

son of: Walter Sarre and Iris Holly Gray
born: 1 August 1941

educated: Adelaide Boys High School, University of Adelaide (LLB) articles with: Howard Zelling QC 1962–1964
admitted: 1964
QC 1982

career: joined independent bar 1982, member Mitchell Chambers 1997–2000, President SA Bar Association 1998–2000, Solicitor-General SA 1979–1986, Chief Counsel Legal Services Commission 1989–1991, Crown Advocate NSW 1987–1989. Justice Supreme Court ACT 2000–2011

married: 1965 Laura 3d 1s

Robert Martin Lunn QC

photo courtesy R M Lunn

son of: Henry Lunn (public servant) and Rae Lunn (home duties)
born: 20 November 1943

educated: Findon and Adelaide High Schools, University of Adelaide (LLB Hons) articles with: L J King QC
admitted: 1966
QC 1983

career: Deputy Master Supreme Court of SA 1972–1976; Master Supreme Court of SA 1984–1989; Judge, District Court of SA 1989–2004; Master Supreme Court of SA 2004–2012. Publications: Author, *Lunn's Civil Procedure South Australia* and *Criminal Law South Australia*.

Thomas Andrew Gray QC

photo courtesy Tom Gray

born: 28 February 1946

educated: St Peters College,
University of Adelaide (LLB Hons)
articles with: Genders Wilson Bray
(Andrew Wilson) admitted: 1969
QC 1984

career: joined independent bar 1982,
member Bar Chambers 1982–2000,
President John Bray Law Chapter
University of Adelaide 2000–2003,
Chair LSSA Advocacy Group
Justice Supreme Court SA 2000–2016

married: 2s 1d Clubs: Adelaide.
Profession interests: legal education.
Numerous publications on legal
topics. Recreation: Tennis, art, travel

Michael Lewis Abbott AO QC

Photo Courtesy Bar Chambers

son of: H L and S L Abbott
born: 23 July 1943

educated: St Peters College, University of Adelaide (LLB) articles with: Dr J J Bray QC admitted: 1966
QC 1984

career: Associate to Justice Leo Travers 1965, joined independent bar 1982, Founder of Wellington Chambers and Market Street Chambers; member of Bar Chambers, Gilles Street Chambers; President SA Bar Association 1997–1999, Chair and Board member Australia India Council since 1993, Inaugural Chair of the Australia Malaysia Institute 1999, Chair Art Gallery SA 2002–2014, Chair Adelaide Festival Trust 2014–2020, Chair Legal Services Commission SA 2013–2020
AO 2011

Recreation: Indian and South East Asian art

David Michael Quick QC

photo courtesy LSSA

son of: F L Quick (Company Secretary & Director) and S C Quick née Higgins (Home Duties)
born: 15 August 1946

educated: St Ignatius College, University of Adelaide (LLB) articles with: R M Duffy 1968–1969
admitted: 3 March 1970
QC 4 October 1984

career: joined independent bar 1977, Part-time Tutor and Lecturer University of Adelaide, Lecturer Hong Kong University, Visiting Associate Professor City University of Hong Kong, (founding) member Hanson Chambers 1977–2001, Adelaide Festival Centre Trust 1986–1997, Council LSSA 1979–1980, Council SA Bar Association, President SA Society of Labour Lawyers, Counsel Assisting Royal Commission: 1) into Shop trading Hours SA 1976–1977, 2) Dismissal of Police Commissioner 1978, 3) Floodlighting at Football Park 1979, 4) Social Security Prosecutions 1984–1985; Marker Judge Advocate's Panel, Australian Defence Force 1985–2002; Defence Force Magistrate 1997–2002, member Howard Zelling Chambers 2003–2008

married: 11 May 1974 Judith Margaret née Tonkin Clubs: Naval Military & Air Force, Mount Osmond Golf

Brian Ross Martin QC

photo courtesy LSSA

son of: Stanley Keith Martin and Neeta Jean Martin (apple orchardists) born: 2 September 1947

educated: Oakbank Area, Adelaide High, University of Adelaide (LLB) articles with: John Mangan, Wallman & Partners 1968–1969 admitted: 1970 QC 1984

career: joined independent bar 1985, member Murray Chambers 1985–1999, Snr Counsel Assisting WA Royal Commission (WA Inc.) 1991–1992, Crown Prosecutor SA 1982–1985, Commonwealth Director of Public Prosecutions 1997–1999, Justice Supreme Ct SA 1999–2004, Chief Justice Supreme Court NT 2004–2010

married: 1969 Leigh Anne 1s 1d
Recreation: sport, travel

Geoffrey Alexander Hackett-Jones QC

photo courtesy LSSA

son of: Frank Harold Hackett-Jones (lawyer) and Mary Gweneth Hackett-Jones (nurse)

born: 17 March 1944, 29 died June 2015

educated: Cowra High School (NSW), Prince Alfred College, University of Adelaide (LLB) articles with: R M Napier QC 1965 admitted: 1967 QC 1986

career: joined independent bar 1988, Associate to Justice Walters 1966, Parliamentary Counsel SA Government 1967–retirement

married: 1973 Clubs: Naval, Military & Air Force
amateur oboist

Brian Robert Michael Hayes QC

photo courtesy Brian Hayes

son of: Henry Robert and Joan Marie Hayes
born: 13 July 1944

educated: St Joseph's College (Darjeeling, India), Marshalswick School (St Albans, Herts, UK), London University articles with: Ian Leckie, Ottaways Solicitors (St Albans, Herts, UK) 1967–1970 admitted: 1971
QC 1986

career: joined independent bar 1984, (founding) member Murray Chambers since 1984, Tutor University of Adelaide 1971, Foundation Advisory Board Member UniSA Law School, Assoc. Professor University of SA (part–time lecturer in Planning Law); Chairman SACON International; Senior Counsel assisting Auditor-General Inquiry into State Bank 1992; Dep. Chair Legal Practitioners Disciplinary Tribunal since 2002, Australian Bar Council; ACH Group board; SA Government Special Envoy to India and Strategic Advisor on India 2008–2018

married: 1970 Gillian 1s 2d

Michael David QC

photo courtesy LSSA

son of: Harry and June David born: 25 October 1944

educated: Rostrevor College, University of Adelaide (LLB) articles with: 1968 Stevens Jacks Mellor & Bollen admitted: 1969
QC 1986

career: joined Independent bar 1973, member Bar Chamber 1973–1996 (mainly criminal work), Judge District Court SA 1996–2006; Justice Supreme Court SA 2006–2014.

married: 1982, Rosemary Clubs: Naval & Military Club, Adelaide University Cricket Club, Adelaide District Cricket Club

Bruce Thomas Lander QC

photo courtesy LSSA

son of: George Lander and Shylie Hamilton Taylor

born: 13 November 1946

educated: Unley High, University of Adelaide (LLB) articles with: Baker McEwin & Co., 1967–1969 admitted: 1969 QC 1986 career: joined independent bar 1982, member Jeffcott Chambers 1982–1994, Legal Practitioners Disciplinary Tribunal, Chair Legal Practitioners Complaints Committee, Justice Supreme Court SA 1994–2003, Federal Court 2003–2013, Inaugural Independent Commissioner Against Corruption 2013–2020

married: 1968 Elizabeth 3d 1s Clubs: Adelaide Recreation: reading, watching football and gardening

John Ronald Mansfield QC

photo courtesy LSSA

born: 25 August 1946

educated: St Ignatius College, University of Adelaide (LLB Hons)
articles with: 1) John Kelly, 2) John Perry, Kelly & Co. admitted: 1969
QC 1986

career: joined independent bar 1979, Hanson Chambers 1982–1996, Tutor in Law 1970–1974, President SA Bar Association 1988–1989, Chairman Legal Aid Committee Law Council of Australia 1986–1994, Counsel in Royal Commission into the State Bank 1991–1993, President Law Council of Australia 1993–1994, President Law Society SA 1988–1989
Justice Federal Court 1996–2016

married: 1972 2s 2d

Malcolm Lindsay Robertson QC

photo courtesy LSSA

son of: Catherine and Herbert Robertson

born: 25 September 1940 educated: Pulteney Grammar, University of Adelaide (LLB) articles with: Nicholas Birchall 1962, Maurice O'Loughlin 1963 admitted: 1964 QC 1986

career: Lecturer in Tax Law University of SA and LSSA, Chairman Taxation Institute of Australia (SA) 1978–1980, National President of Taxation Institute of Australia 1980–1981, joined independent bar 1982, Judge District Ct SA 1996–2010

married: 1965 Helen 3d Clubs: Kooyonga Golf Recreation: golf, reading, wine appreciation, history

Robert David Lawson QC

photo courtesy Robert Lawson

son of: Charles Lawson (accountant) and Kathleen E Lawson
born: 15 August 1944

educated: Adelaide High, St Marks College, University of Adelaide (LLB)
articles with: Fisher Jeffries & Co.,
admitted: 1968
QC 1988

career: joined independent bar 1982, member Jeffcott Chambers since 1982, Counsel in Royal Commission into the Dismissal of Harold Salisbury 1978, Counsel in Royal Commission into the State Bank of SA 1991–1992, President SA Bar Association 1990–1992, Jnr Vice-President Australian Bar Association 1991–1992, Minister Consumer Affairs, 2001–2002, Workplace Services 2001–2002, Disability Services and the Aging 2001–2002
SA Attorney-General 2001–2002, SA Dep. Leader Opposition in the Legislative Council since 2002, Opposition Attorney-General since 2002

married: 1970 Delysia 1s 1d Clubs: Adelaide, Naval Military and Air Force, Royal Adelaide Golf

Timothy Russell Anderson QC

Photo courtesy Tim Anderson

son of: Allan James Anderson, journalist and Molly Patricia Anderson, home duties
born: 4 July 1945

educated: St Ignatius College, University of Adelaide (LLB) articles with: Ward Mollison Litchfield Ward 1968, Ward and Partners 1969
admitted: 1970
QC 1988

career: joined independent bar 1977, Founding member Hanson Chambers 1977–2003; Acting Judge Licensing Court 1982; Counsel State Bank Royal Commission, Deputy Chairman Drug and Alcohol Services; Chairperson Legal Practitioners Disciplinary Tribunal; Enquiries for SA Govt into Liquor Licensing and Ministerial Misconduct
Justice Supreme Court of South Australia 2003–2014
President, Racing Appeals Tribunal since 2014; Review of the *Liquor Licensing Act 1997* 2016; Review of gambling regulations 2017; Inaugural Chair, State Planning Commission 2018–2019; commercial mediations since 2014

married: 1968 Clubs: Norwood Football Club

Terence Anthony Worthington QC

photo courtesy LSSA

son of: Norman Alfred and Iris Mary Worthington
born: 24 April 1943

educated: CBC Manly (NSW), Sacred Heart College (SA), University of Adelaide (LLB) articles with: J R Kearnan QC and W A N Wells QC Crown Solicitor 1967–1968
admitted: 1969
QC 1988

career: joined independent bar 1985, Board Examiners Supreme Court 1983–1986, President Law Society SA 1985–1986, Chairman Legal Services Commission 1986–1995, State Bank Royal Commission Senior Counsel for SGIC, Inquiry into Allegations of Conflict of Interest re Minister of Tourism 1992 (Wiese Inquiry), Judge District Court SA 1995
Chief Judge District Court SA 1997–2013

married: 1970 Jill 4s 1d

Barry Jennings QC

photo courtesy Barry Jennings

son of: Jack Jennings (ALP MP 1953–1977) and Barbara Jennings
born: 8 August 1946

educated: Blackfriars Priory School, University of Adelaide (LLB) articles with: Crown Solicitor SA admitted: 1970
QC 1988

career: Crown Prosecutor 1979–1982; independent bar 1984–1985; Chief Counsel Legal Services Commission 1985–1989; Crown Counsel 1989–1995
Judge District Court SA 1995
Chief Judge Youth Court SA 1996–2006

married: Margaret Recreation: SACA and Crows

Sydney William Tilmouth QC

photo courtesy Sydney Tilmouth

born: 5 February 1950

educated: Marion High, University of Adelaide (BA, LLB) articles with: Chris Cocks 1972 admitted: 1973
QC 1989

career: joined independent bar 1975, Faculty Member Australian Institute Trial Advocacy and National Institute Trial Advocacy America, teaches advocacy across Australia, Bangladesh, Singapore and America, Royal Commission into Prisons 1979, Royal Commission into Hindmarsh Island 1995–1996, director Legal Services Commission 1985–1987, Edmund Barton Chambers 1989–2005; Publications: *Australian Criminal Trial Directions* ongoing, *Advocacy in Practice* 1998 (co-author)
Judge District Court SA 2005–2020, Auxiliary Judge Supreme Court SA since 2017

divorced 2 children Interests bush walking, travel, reading

Geoffrey Michael Eames QC

photo courtesy LSSA

son of: John Alexander Eames, fitter, and Mary Elizabeth Eames, secretary and home duties
born: 26 November 1945

educated: St Bernard's College, Essendon, Victoria; University of Melbourne (LLB) articles with: Slater & Gordon (Victoria) 1968 admitted: 1969 (Vic.) 1980 (SA)
QC 1989 (SA) 1990 (Vic.)

career: joined independent bar 1984, member Hanson Chambers 1987–1991, Royal Commission into British Nuclear Tests (Maralinga) 1985, Royal Commission into Aboriginal Deaths in Custody 1987–1991, Chair AIJA Jury Charges Committee, Chair Judicial Officers Aboriginal Cultural Awareness Committee
Justice Supreme Court of Victoria 1992–2002, Justice Court of Appeal Victoria 2002–2015

married: 1968 Patricia

William Jonathan Noye Wells QC

photo courtesy Hanson Chambers

son of: Andrew Wells AO QC (Justice Supreme Court SA 1970–1984) and Eleanor Wells (née Jacobs; social worker, founding member CAB)
born: 29 January 1951

educated: St Peters College, University of Adelaide (LLB) Oxford University (BCL) articles with: D.W. Bollen QC
admitted: 1975
QC 1990

career: joined independent bar 1979, Part-time lecturer and examiner University of Adelaide, Chair Administrative Law Committee LSSA 1988–1989, Criminal Law Committee LSSA 1997–2000, Chair Legal Education Committee LSSA 1985–1989, Dep. Chair Legal Advisory Committee LSSA since 1994, President SA Bar Association 2003–2004, Co-trustee Julian Centre, co-founder of JusticeNet SA Inc. and founding member of the management board; Honorary member of the Law Society of SA; Justice Award, Law Society of SA 2009; member of Hanson Chambers since 1979, current Head

married: 1977 Jane Elizabeth Wreford (teacher) (dec. 2002)

John Robert Sulan QC

photo courtesy LSSA

son of: Charles Sulan (accountant) and Roszi Sulan (secondary school teacher)
born: 28 April 1946

educated: Norwood High, Pulteney Grammar, University of Adelaide (LLB)
articles with: Graham Olsson 1967
admitted: 1969
QC 1990

career: Associate to Justice Walters 1968–1969, Publications: SA editor *Cross on Evidence* 1969–1970, Assisted in updating *Wells on Evidence* 1969, joined independent bar 1991, Bar Chambers 1990–1997; from 2016 Lecturer Law Society SA, Chairperson Law Society Professional Development Committee, Chairperson Jewish Community Services, Special Investigation into collapse of Bond Corporation Ltd, Chairman Flinders Technologies PL 1995–1997
Governor's Multi Cultural Award Outstanding Individual Achievement 2013
Judge District Court SA 1997–2003
Justice Supreme Court SA 2003–2016
Reviewer of the Independent Commissioner Against Corruption since 2019

Neville Wayne Morcombe QC

photo courtesy LSSA

son of: Andrew Morcombe and Gladys Jean Willis born: 20 January 1949

educated: Adelaide Technical High, University of Adelaide (LLB) articles with: Baker McEwin 1970–1971
admitted: 1971
QC 1991

career: joined independent bar 1985, member Campbell Chambers 1985–1999, Edmund Barton Chambers since 1999, Australian Army 1972–1974 (National Service), Army Reserves 1974–2017, Reserve Force Decoration 1987, Counsel Assisting Army Board of Inquiry (BOI) into death of Australian soldier in Malaysia 1998–1999, Counsel Assisting Army BOI into death of Australian soldier in USA 2002–2003, Judge Advocate and Defence Force Magistrate 1989–2007, President Law Society SA 1991–1992, Colonel Australian Army Reserve, National Service Medal 2002 Legal Practitioners Discipline Tribunal from 1995 to 2010 (Presiding member 2004–2010)

married: 1971 Pamela 2d, 1982 Jane 3s, 1999 Robbie, 2012 Julie

Stephen Walsh QC

photo courtesy EBC

son of: Joseph Walsh and Winifred Oakes
born: 23 March 1950

educated: St Ignatius College, University of Adelaide (LLB)
admitted: 1973
QC 1991

career: joined independent bar 1992, Edmund Barton Chambers since 1996; Councillor and Alderman City of Burnside 1977–1987, President Law Society SA 1993–1994, Chair Environment Protection Authority SA Govt 1994–2003, President Institute Justice Studies 1998

Paul John Lawrence Rofe QC

photo courtesy LSSA

son of: Bryan Rofe (school teacher, scientist, director of Antarctic Division) and Patricia Rofe (school teacher and home duties)
born: 20 January 1948 died 7 May 2013

educated: St Ignatius College, Norwood; University of Adelaide (LLB) articles with: Peter Allan 1973 admitted: 1973
QC 1991

career: 1974 Judge's Associate to Justice George Walters and Chief Justice John Bray, joined independent bar 1993, Board National Criminal Courts Statistics Unit, Australian Bureau of Statistics; National Committee for Child Sexual Abuse Reform, Director of Public Prosecutions (formerly Crown Prosecutor) 1991–2004; Elliott Johnston Chambers 2004–2013.

Clubs: Director Adelaide Football Club 1999–2003

David Frank Wicks QC

photo courtesy LSSA

born: 18 February 1939 died 16 February 2012

educated: Prince Alfred College, University of Adelaide (LLB) articles with: Pickering Cornish (Tony Abbott)
admitted: 1962
QC 1991

career: President Law Society South Australia 1983–1984, Royal Commission into Commercial Activities and other matters of WA and SA governments 1991–1992, joined independent bar in 1991, founding member of Divett Chambers 1993
Justice Supreme Court SA 1998–2003

married: Orietta Feb 1966, 1s 1d
Clubs: Adelaide

Robyn Ann Layton AO QC

photo courtesy Robyn Layton

born: 16 August 1945

educated: University of Adelaide (LLB, LLM) admitted: 1968
QC 1992

career: joined independent bar 1989, member Murray Chambers since 1990, Judge and Deputy President SA Industrial Court 1978–1985, Counsel in Royal Commission into the Moratorium March, Counsel in Royal Commission into the dismissal of a schoolgirl, Counsel in Royal Commission into the Juvenile Courts System, Solicitor in Royal Commission into Drugs 1977, Chair Human Rights Committee Law Society SA since 1997, Chair Review of Child Protection in SA since 2002 International Labour Office Geneva 1993–2008
Justice of Supreme Court of South Australia 2005–2010
University of SA Adjunct Prof Justice and Society
co–author *Evidence Law*

Catherine Margaret Branson AC QC

photo courtesy Catherine Branson

daughter of: Lewis Max and Barbara Currie Rayner
born: 2 May 1948

educated: Presbyterian Girls College, University of Adelaide (BA, LLB)
articles with: Peter Green admitted: 1974
QC 1992

career: joined independent bar 1989, member Bar Chambers 1989–1994, Crown Solicitor and CEO Attorney-General's Office (SA) 1984–1989, Board Queen Victoria Hospital 1982–1988, President Australian Institute Judicial Administration 1998–2000, Council University of SA 1992–1996, Law School University of Adelaide 1989–1993; Adj Prof since 2013 Justice Federal Court of Australia 1994–2008, President Australian Human Rights Commission 2009–2012, Human Rights Commissioner 2009–2012, Chair Human Rights Law Centre since 2016 LLD (hon.) Flinders University 2012, Doctor of Letters (hon.) Macquarie University 2014 Chancellor University of Adelaide from July 2020
2018 AC

Dean Ernest Clayton QC

photo courtesy LSSA

son of: Ernest Clarence and Renie Florence Clayton
born: 17 April 1943

educated: Adelaide Boys High School, University of Adelaide (LLB) articles with: Johnston & Olsson admitted: 1966
QC 1992

career: assoc. to Hon. Justice Hogarth, joined independent bar 1988, member Bar Chambers 1988–2003, President Law Society SA 1994–1995, Royal Commission: "The Motorola Report" Judge District Court of South Australia 2003–2013

married: 1964 Julia Brendish 3s 1d Clubs: Adelaide, Kooyonga Golf Recreation: golf, rowing, snow skiing, wine

Belinda (Lindy) Jane Powell QC

photo courtesy LSSA

born: 30 March 1952

educated: Walford Church of England Girls School, University of Adelaide (LLB) articles with: John Perry Kelly & Co. admitted: 1973
QC 1994

career: Judge's Associate 1974 Dame Roma Mitchell, Chairman, Legal Committee and Council Member SA Child Protection Council 1988–1991, Director SA Legal Services Commission 1987–1991, joined independent bar 1991, member Bar Chambers since 1991, President Law Society SA 1998–1999, Bd Examiners Supreme Ct SA 1999–2001

Anthony James Besanko QC

Photo courtesyAnthony Besanko

son of: L S Besanko and M M O'Connell
born: 8 May 1954

educated: St Ignatius College, University of Adelaide (LLB Hons I) articles with: Ward & Partners
admitted: 1978
QC 1994

career: Ward & Partners 1977–1983; joined independent bar 1984, Member of Murray Chambers (1984–1985), Jeffcott Chambers 1985–2001; President SA Bar Association 2000–2001; Member Law Society Council; Member and then Presiding Member Legal Practitioners Disciplinary Tribunal; Member of the Legal Practitioners Education and Admissions Council; Member of the Law Admissions Consultative Committee; Director and Fellow of the Australian Academy of Law; Judicial Fellowship at the University of London (January–March 2020)

Justice Supreme Court of South Australia 2001–2006, Additional Justice Supreme Court of the Australian Capital Territory since 2007; Justice Supreme Court of Norfolk Island 2013–2015; Chief Justice Supreme Court of Norfolk Island since 2015
Justice Federal Court Australia since 2006

married: 1980 Andrea Kirstyn Harley
2s 1d

Bradley Maxwell Selway QC

photo courtesy LSSA

son of: Vernon and Dawn Selway
born: 9 January 1955, died 10 April 2005

educated: Westminster School (Marion), University of Adelaide (LLB)
articles with: G C Prior QC, Crown Solicitor's Office 1977 admitted: 1978
QC 1994

career: Crown Solicitor 1989–1995, Solicitor-General 1995–2002, Adjunct Professor of Law, University of Adelaide 2002–2005, Publications: The Constitution of SA (1997), *Government in Law of Australia* (co–author, 1994), *Public Law and the South Australian Crown* (1990) Justice Federal Court 2003–2005

married: 1976 Christine 2d Clubs: Adelaide, South Adelaide Football Club, SACA, Rotary

Ann Marie Vanstone QC

photo courtesy LSSA

daughter of: Bartley James and Joan Nancy Vanstone

educated: Walford Church of England Girls Grammar School, Presbyterian Girls College articles with: Cleland & Co. admitted: 7 February 1978
QC 1994

career: joined independent bar 1994, Christopher Legoe Chambers 1994–1999; Judge District Court SA 1999–2003, Justice Supreme Court SA 2003–2019, SA Independent Commissioner Against Corruption from 2020 (Sep.)

Gordon Fraser Barrett QC

photo courtesy Gordon Barrett

born: 26 March 1949

educated: Scotch College; University of Adelaide (LLB; BA) articles with: Cleland Teasdale Smith & Co. (Michael Cleland) admitted: 1971
QC 1996

career: 1979 Royal Commission into Prisons (Co–Counsel for prisoners); joined independent bar 1983, Member Wellington Chambers, Market Street Chambers, founding member Mitchell Chambers 1991, Correctional Services Advisory Council, Legal Services Commission, Refugee Advocacy Service of South Australia; Judge, District Court of South Australia 2005–2019.

Robert (Dick) John Whitington QC

photo courtesy LSSA

born: 5 February 1950

admitted: 1979
QC 1996

career: joined independent bar 1985; Hanson Chambers since 1988.

Darrell Alfred Trim QC

photo courtesy Darrell Trim

born: 6 November 1944

educated: Prince Alfred College, University of Adelaide (LLB Hons)
articles with: Mohr Birchall & Co., Birchall Stratford & Co. 1966–1967
admitted: 1968
QC 1996

career: joined independent bar 1984, Torrens Chambers 1984–2018, Murray Chambers from 2018; Board of Examiners Supreme Court since 2002

married: Valerie 3s 2d Clubs: Mt Barker Golf

Marie Elizabeth Shaw QC

photo courtesy Marie Shaw

born: 16 August 1952

educated: Loreto College, University of Adelaide (LLB) 1974 articles with: Moran & McRae 1975–1976
admitted: 1976
QC 1996

career: joined independent bar 1985, Counsel to Aboriginal Legal Rights Movement 1987–1989, Human Rights & Equal Opportunity Commission since 1999, Chairperson Criminal Law Committee LSSA since 2001, Chief Counsel Legal Services 2004–2005; Judge District Court of South Australia 2005–2010.

Married: 3 children Recreation: Past State coach YCW netball, tennis

Steven Albert Millsteed QC

photo courtesy Steven Millsteed

son of: Shirley and Ted Millsteed
born: 18 August 1953

educated: Unley High School, University of Adelaide (LLB) articles with: Wallman & Partners 1976
admitted: 1976
QC 1996

career: joined independent bar 2003, Bar Chambers 2003–2004; Judge District Court 2004–2018

married: 1995 Recreation: music, reading, squash, basketball

Richard Conway White QC

photo courtesy Richard White

son of: E N and N K White
born: 6 January 1952

educated: University of Adelaide (LLB, BA) articles with: David Quick, Stanley and Partners 1976 admitted: 1977
QC 1997

career: Stanley & Partners 1979–1982; joined independent bar 1982; Council Law Society SA 1989–1993 (Professional Conduct and Practice Committee 1992–1993, Professional Indemnity Committee 1993–1996); Litigation Assistance Advisory Board 1992–1993; Board of Examiners Supreme Court SA 1999–2004; Legal Practitioners Disciplinary Committee 2000–2004 and Chairperson 2003–2004, Chairperson Classification of Publications Board SA 1986–1993
Justice Supreme Court SA 2004–2013
Justice Federal Court since 2013

married: 1978 Carmel

Christopher John Kourakis SC

photo courtesy Christopher Kourakis

son of: Evangelos and Roxani Kourakis
born: 17 June 1958

educated: Port Lincoln High,
University of Adelaide (LLB Hons.)
articles with: Johnston Withers
McCusker 1982 admitted: 1982
QC 1997; SC 2008

career: joined independent bar
1996, member Edmund Barton
Chambers 1996–2003, Legal Services
Commission 1993–1999, President
Law Society SA 2001–2003, Solicitor-
General SA 2003–2008
Justice Supreme Court SA 2008–2012,
Chief Justice since 2012

married: 1981 Valerie Germanos 3d

Wendy Jane Abraham QC

Photo courtesy Wendy Abraham

parents: Janet and Joseph Abraham (accountant)
born: 7 May 1960

educated: Loreto College, University of Adelaide (LLB Honours), Graduate Diploma of Legal Practice admitted: 1982
QC 1998

career: SA Office of Director of Public Prosecutions (then Crown Prosecutor's Office) 1983–2005; Assoc. Director of Public Prosecutions (SA) 1995–May 2004; Acting Director of Public Prosecutions May 2004–May 2005; joined the New South Wales Bar in 2005 on full time retainer as national appellate counsel for the Commonwealth Director of Public Prosecution; 12 Wentworth/ Selborne Chambers 2009–2019, NSW (with a national appellate practice). Committees include: Executive Committee, International Association of Prosecutors: 2002–2008; Professional Conduct Committee (NSW Bar Association) 2015–2019, Chair 2018–2019; NSW Silks selection committee 2017, (NSW Bar Association). Consultations include: Victorian Parliament Law Reform Committee – DNA, 2002; the Australian Law Reform Commission – DNA, 2002 Member, Advisory Committee to the Australian Law Reform Commission Corporate Crime Inquiry 2019–2020

Justice Federal Court Australia since 7 May 2019

David William Smith QC

photo courtesy LSSA

son of: William Lott Smith (publican) and Mary Josephine (home duties) born: 5 March 1945

educated: Rostrevor College, University of Adelaide (LLB) articles with: Stevens Jacobs Mellor & Bollen 1967–1969 admitted: 1969 QC 1998

career: joined independent bar 1983, Counsel assisting the Royal Commission into SA prisons for Port Augusta 1981, Counsel assisting the Hindmarsh Island Bridge Royal Commission 1995, District Court SA 1999–2015

married: 1970 Mary Clubs: Royal Adelaide Golf, Grange Golf

Steven Andrew Strickland QC

photo courtesy LSSA

son of: Graham Proctor and Nora Strickland
born: 20 November 1951

educated: Plympton High, University of Adelaide (LLB Hons) articles with: Wallman & Partners (Malcolm Montgomery) 1973 admitted: 1973 QC 1998

career: Tutor in Property, Lecturer in Succession, University of Adelaide; Lecturer in Law of Education, SA Institute of Technology, joined independent bar 1985, Chair Organising Committee 6th National Family Law Conference 1994, Campbell Chambers 1984–1999; Justice Family Court since 1999

married: 1987 Marina 2d

David Malcolm Haines QC

photo courtesy LSSA

son of: Edwin James Haines (clerk) and Anne Haines (home duties) born: 13 August 1944 died 2013

educated: Brighton High School, University of Adelaide (LLB; LLM 1989) articles with: Athol Olsson (1 year), Max Basheer (3 years) admitted: 1971 QC 1999

career: joined independent bar 1987, member Edmund Barton Chambers 1987–2005, Howard Zelling Chambers since 2005, Occasional lecturer in Succession Flinders University, written extensively and given papers on Family Law and Succession publication: *Succession Law in South Australia* 2003. Clubs: Adelaide

Kevin Vincent Borick QC

photo credit LSSA

son of: Richard and Mabel Borick
born: 7 August 1937

educated: Rostrevor College, University of Adelaide (LLB) articles with: H E Zelling QC admitted: 1960 QC 1999 career: joined independent bar 1973, member Libra/Cleland Chambers 1973–2002, Sir Mellis Napier Chambers 2002–2003.

married: Susan J Davies

David Harvey Peek QC

photo courtesy LSSA

son of: Donald (pharmacist) and Mavis Peek
born: 3 April 1952

educated: University of Adelaide (LLB), University of Tasmania (LLM)
admitted: 1976
QC 1999

career: Tutor University of Adelaide, joined independent bar 1982, member Jeffcott Chambers 1982–1990, Acting Magistrate mid–1980s, Murray Chambers 1990–2010, Criminal Law Committee of LSSA (past chair) Justice Supreme Court SA since 2010

Clubs: South Australian Fly Fishers.
Motto: "Have Lunn. Will travel."

Andrew Robert Harris QC

photo courtesy Andrew Harris

son of: Robert Eric Harris (stock agent) and Margaret Harris (home duties)
born: 11 March 1956

educated: Westminster School, University of Adelaide (LLB) articles with: Ross Duffy (Wallmans) 1979
admitted: 1980
QC 1999

career: joined independent bar 1982, (founding) member Jeffcott Chambers since 1982; SA Bar Association Council member 2002–2018, President SA Bar Association 2014–2016; Australian Bar Association Council member 2014–2018

married: 1982 Bronwen 3d; 2010 Elizabeth 1s Clubs: Adelaide, Royal Adelaide Golf Recreation: Alpine skiing, water skiing, golf, tennis, photography, reading, travel

Paul John Rice QC

photo courtesy LSSA

son of: William (Bill) Rice (pharmacist) and Marg Rice (home duties)
born: 5 November 1949

educated: Blackfriars Priority School, University of Adelaide (LLB) articles with: Roder Dunstan Lee & Taylor 1971 admitted: 1972
QC 1999

career: Judge's Associate to John Bray 1972–1973, joined independent bar 1989, member Edmund Barton Chambers 1989–1994, Crown Prosecutor 1985–1988, judge District Ct SA 2000–2019

married: 1989 Rosey Davey (Judge District Court SA 2009–2016)

Malcolm Fraser Blue QC

photo courtesy LSSA

son of: Norman Hannah Blue (public servant) and Patricia Agness Blue (Nursing Sister)
born: 12 August 1954

educated: Kings College (1971), University of Adelaide (LLB Hons.)
articles with: Commonwealth Crown Solicitor 1976–1977 admitted: 1977
QC 2001

career: joined independent bar 1996, member Bar Chambers 1996–2011
Justice Supreme Court SA since 2011

Recreations: TSOA, swimming, music

Philip Anthony McNamara QC

photo courtesy Philip McNamara

born: 21 December 1949

educated: St Edmunds Christian Brothers College (Canberra), ANU (LLB), McGill (MCL) articles with: Dare Reed Martin & Grant, Sydney, 1972. admitted: 1981
QC 2001

career: Tutored at Macquarie University, McGill University, University of Adelaide; joined independent bar 1984, member of Murray Chambers 1990–2014, SABA Committee ca 1987–1992; Editorial Panel Australian Mining & Petroleum Law Association ca 1983–1990; Editorial Panel *Australian Bar Review*.

Paul Anthony Heywood-Smith QC

photo courtesy Paul Heywood–Smith

son of: Delbridge Heywood-Smith and Constance Heylen
born: 2 September 1949

educated: Prince Alfred College, University of Adelaide (LLB Hons)
articles with: Elliott Johnston QC 1972
admitted: 1973 (SA), 1976 (UK)
QC 2002

career: occasional lecturer, Flinders University Law School; former Chairperson, now Patron of the Australian Friends of Palestine (AFOPA); joined independent bar 1996, publications: *The Case for Palestine*, Wakefield Press; *Ratowa, A House by the Sea*; (founding) member Divett Chambers 1993, Anthony Mason Chambers since 2006

married: Edie Bransbury
memberships: Prince Alfred College Foundation, St Mark's College
recreation: painting

Michael Thomas Boylan QC

photo courtesy Michael Boylan

son of: Francis Eugene Boylan (Barrister; Judge District Court) and Nellie Patricia Boylan)
born: 30 September 1951

educated: St Ignatius College, University of Adelaide (LLB) articles with: J W Perry (q.v.)
admitted: 1974 QC 2002

career: associate to Hon. Justice J.M. White 1978–1980, Assisted Crown Prosecutor 1982–1990, joined independent bar 1990, member Edmund Barton Chambers 1990–2004, Judge District Court SA since 7 October 2004

married: 21 March 1981 Deborah Glasgow née Morgan

Barry Francis Beazley QC

photo courtesy *The Advertiser*

son of: Francis William and Ursula Beazley
born: 4 April 1951 (Wagga Wagga)

educated: Christian Brothers (Wagga Wagga), St Kilda (Melbourne) University of Adelaide (LLB Hons)
articles with: Povey, Waterhouse & Basheer 1975 admitted: 1975
QC 2002

career: Part–time tutor University of Adelaide 1976–1982, joined independent bar 1989, Member Edmund Barton Chambers 1989–2005, Chair SA National Football League Disciplinary Tribunal 1990–2002, Chairman Independent Gaming Corporation 1999–2002 Judge District Court SA 2005–2020

married: Sara, 3 ch. Clubs: South Australian National Football League (Life member), South Australian Cricket Association

David Cameron Lovell QC

photo courtesy David Lovell

born: 17 February 1955

educated: Prince Alfred College, University of Adelaide (LLB) articles with: Martin & Co. 1977 admitted: 1978
QC 2002

career: Senior Assistant Prosecutor, Crown Prosecution Office 1983–1989; joined independent bar 1990, member Jeffcott Chambers 1990–2015; President Racing Appeals Tribunal 1994–2006; Counsel representing various interests Royal Commission: 1) State Bank, 2) Hindmarsh Island 3) Kapunda Road
Judge District Court SA 2006–2015
Justice Supreme Court SA since 2015

married: (2) 1995 Margaret Clubs: Royal Adelaide Golf Recreation: Cricket (Represented SA 1979–1981), Bradman Medal 1978/79, runner–up 1979/80, reading, golf, photography

Patricia Kelly QC

photo courtesy LSSA

daughter of: Gabrielle and Michael Kelly
born: 6 January 1952

educated: Cabra Dominican College, University of Adelaide (LLB) articles with: Clement O'Sullivan (Darwin), Justice W J Forster (Supreme Court, Darwin) admitted: 1974
QC 2002

career: Director of Public Prosecutions SA Judge District Court SA 2003–2007 Justice Supreme Court SA since 2007

Paul Vincent Slattery QC

photo courtesy *The Advertiser*

son of: John Vincent Slattery (manager) and Kathleen Patricia Slattery (secretary/personal assistant)
born: 18 February 1955

educated: Sacred Heart College, University of Adelaide (LLB) articles with: Anthony B Fuller (O'Loughlin Robertson & Co.) 1978 admitted: 1979
QC 2003

career: joined independent bar 1994, 1982–1989 LSSA Civil Litigation Committee, Litigation Assistance Fund Advisory Board 1999–2010, South Australian Gas Review Board
Judge District Court SA since 2012

married: 1980 Andrea Elizabeth (née Murdoch) Clubs: Adelaide, Kooyonga Golf

Peter Robert Brebner QC

photo courtesy LSSA

son of: Charles Brebner (solicitor) and Joyce Brebner (home duties)
born: 16 November 1948

educated: Prince Alfred College, University of Adelaide (LLB) articles with: Fisher Jeffries (Gordon Gratton)
admitted: 1975
QC 2003

career: Judge's Associate to Justice Keith Sangster and Chief Justice John Bray; President, Athletics SA 1984–1986, Crown Prosecutor since 1978 Judge District Court of SA 2008–2018

Recreation: Golf, Reading

Paul Andrew Cuthbertson QC

photo courtesy LSSA

son of: Kenneth John Mackenzie Cuthbertson (grazier) and Pauline Eugenie Cuthbertson (home duties) born: 10 March 1953

educated: Prince Alfred College, University of Adelaide (LLB) articles with: Ward & Partners 1975 (Terry Worthington) admitted: 1976 QC 2003

career: joined independent bar 1987, tutor in Advocacy training, Advocacy Committee, member Edmund Barton Chambers 1987–2009 Judge District Court SA since 2009

married: Fiona née Callaghan 17 February 2001 Clubs: Naval Military & Airforce, League Commissioner SANFL

Michael David Walter QC

photo courtesy LSSA

son of: Rex and Gloria Walter (both teachers)
born: 15 May 1945

educated: Findon High, University of Adelaide (LLB) articles with: Graham Prior QC Crown Solicitor admitted: 1981 QC 2003 career: Flight Lieutenant RAAF 1971–1975, Tutor in Torts University of Adelaide 1980–1981, Crown Solicitor 1996–2004

Clubs: Grange Golf Club

Dr Melissa Anne Perry QC

photo courtesy Melissa Perry

daughter of: Jennifer Mary and the Hon. Justice John Perry AO QC

educated: Walford CEGGS, University of Adelaide (LLB Hons), University of Cambridge (LLM, Phd), David Murray Scholarship (University of Adelaide), Shell Cambridge Scholarship, Yorke Prize (University of Cambridge), admitted 1985 (SA), 1999 (NSW), 2012 (England and Wales)
QC 2004

career: joined SA independent bar 1992, Inner Temple 2012; Council member, St Marks College 1995–2000; Joint Chair, Constitutional Law Sub–Committee, Law Society of South Australia 2003–2004; member, Legal Practitioners Education and Admission Council 2004–2006; Law Council of Australia, Administrative Law Sub–Committee 2005–2012; member, Human Rights Committee 2010–2013 and Equal Opportunity Committee 2011–2012, NSW Bar Association; Australian Association of Constitutional Law, Council member 1998–2005, Secretary 2005–2008; Administrative Review Council 2006–2013; Visiting Research Fellow, Lauterpacht Centre for International Law at the University of Cambridge 2005–2006; member, Law School Advisory Board, University of Adelaide since 2006; Foundation Fellow since 2009 and former Director, Australian Academy of Law; member, Advisory Committee, Gilbert + Tobin Centre of Public Law, UNSW since 2011; Royal Australian Air Force Legal Specialist Reserves since 2011; member, Board of Advisors, Research Unit on Military Law and Ethics University of Adelaide since 2014; section-editor, *Australian Law Journal* since 2014; member, Advisory Council, Centre for International and Public Law, ANU (since 2015); Federal Court representative, Judicial Council on Cultural Diversity since 2014; Patron, NSW Chapter of the Hellenic Australian Lawyers Association since 2016. Judge, Federal Court of Aus since 2013; Additional Judge, Supreme Court ACT since 2014; Deputy President, Administrative Appeals Tribunal since 2018; Member, Defence Force Discipline Appeals Tribunal since 2018.

Publications: Perry and Lloyd (eds), *Australian Native Title Law (2nd Ed)* (Thomsons Law Book Co, 2019); *Disqualification of Judges: Practice and Procedure: Discussion Paper* (Australian Institute of Judicial Administration, 2001)

Recreation: Music; reading, travel, writing, exercise and public speaking.

Maurine Pyke QC

photo courtesy Maurine Pyke

Daughter of: Geoffrey Patrick Pyke (Life Insurance) and Eileen Jean Pyke (Clerical)
born: 15 June 1951

educated: St Dominic's Priory College, University of Adelaide (LLB) articles with: Doreen Davey.
Admitted: December 1973
QC 2004

career: joined independent bar 1986, John Bray Chambers since 1991. Family Law Section LSSA; President, Central Eastern Domestic Violence Service; SABA Executive; Legal Services Commissioner; Observer, Family Law Council Royal Commissions: Hindmarsh Island Member, Disciplinary Tribunal Legal Practitioners.

Recreation: Opera, theatre, golf, gym, travel.

Mark Andrew Griffin QC

photo courtesy Mark Griffin

Son of: John Anthony (Tony) dec'd (Operations Manager) and Patricia Elizabeth Griffin (home duties)
born: 4 April 1957 died Dec 2019

educated: St Ignatius College, University of Adelaide (LLB) articles with: John Goldberg. Admitted: December 1979
QC 2006

career: Wright Chambers 1997–2009, 2012–2019 Clinical Instructor, Boston College Law School 1993,1994,1995; Advocacy instructing, LSSA since 1991
Judge District Court SA 2009–2012

Married: Lesley 1999 1s Recreation: Member and legal advisor Port Adelaide Football Club, playing any sport. 'Luckiest and happiest guy I know! Successful liver transplant early 2006'

Mark Cameron James Hoffmann QC

photo courtesy Mark Hoffmann

Son of: Dr D C Hoffmann OAM (surgeon) and Margaret A Hoffmann
born: 2 June 1963

educated: Prince Alfred College, University of Adelaide (LLB Hons);
Admitted: SA 1987; Hong Kong 2017
QC 2006

career: Associate to Justice Matheson and Justice Cox; Tutor, Bachelor of Business; Partner, Fisher Jeffries 1991–2002; Board of Examiners; Bar Chambers since 2003, Head of Chambers since November 2009; Assoc Member of 9 Selborne Chambers (Sydney) since 2016; President of the SA Bar Assoc from 2018

Recreation: PAC and Scotch Old Scholars Football Clubs, snow skiing, Belmore Ski Club, motorsport, wine, touch football

Mark Christopher Livesey QC

photo courtesy Mark Livesey

Son of: Peter Livesey (company director) and Janette Rae Livesey (home duties)
born: 20 November 1963

educated: Pulteney Grammar School, University of Adelaide (LLB, LLM);
Admitted: December 1986
QC 2006

career: Associate to Justice Mohr 1986–87; Ward and Partners; GDLP; LSSA; Judges Rules Advisory Committee; Bar Chambers since 2003; Kapunda Road Royal Commission President, South Australian Bar Association, 2010–2012
President, Australian Bar Association, 2014–2015 Chairman, Bar Ethics Committee, 2010–2020 Co–Chairman, Forum for Barristers and Advocates, International Bar Association, 2014–2016
International Fellow, International Academy of Trial Lawyers, 2015
Special Investigator, reporting to the Attorney-General on the Procurement of 9 Diesel Emergency Power Generators, 3 April 2018 Fellow, Australian Academy of Law, 2019
Justice Supreme Court and Court of Appeal SA since 2020

Married: Catherine. 3d 6s
Recreation: Woodville West Torrens Football Club, Adelaide Football Club, Art Gallery of SA

Stephen Kevin McEwen QC

photo courtesy Stephen McEwen

Son of: Kevin Maurice McEwen (soldier settler) and Adrienne Mary McEwen (Post Mistress)
born: 12 April 1958 Millicent SA.

educated: Reedy Creek Area School, Marist Bros Mt Gambier, University of Adelaide (LLB); Admitted: December 1981
QC 2006

career: Reilly Ahern and Kerin 1980–1984; Partner Bell and McEwen 1984–1988; LSSA Criminal Law Committee, Advocacy Committee; ODPP 1988–2001; Wright Street Chambers 2001–2005; Auxilliary Judge Youth Court 2005–2006; Senior Judge since 2006

Married: 1981 Recreation: Equestrian – Horse SA, Pony Club, squash, landcare, football

Sashi Jass Maharaj QC

photo courtesy Sashi Maharaj

born: 12 April 1958

educated: St Joseph's Secondary School (Suva, Fiji). University of Tasmania (LLB) articles with: Crown Solicitor, Tasmania. Admitted: December 1983 QC 2006

Associate to Chief Justice of Tasmania, Sir Guy Green; Counsel Commonwealth Crown Solicitor's Office 1983–1997; Murray Chambers 1997–2016, Owen Dixon Chambers (Melbourne) since 2016.

Recreation: travelling, reading, chess, trekking, cooking

Kevin Gordon Nicholson QC

photo courtesy Kevin Nicholson

Son of: Gordon Lewis Edgar and Doreen Patricia Nicholson.
born: 28 March 1953

educated: Narrabeen Boys High School (NSW); Sydney University, Cambridge University articles with: Peter Scammell, Henry Davis York (Sydney). Admitted: 1977 (NSW); 1995 (SA)
QC 2006

career: solicitor, Henry Davis York (Sydney); Lecturer, University of Newcastle 1983–1986; Lecturer, Senior Lecturer, Associate Professor, University of Adelaide Law School 1987–1997; Consultant Piper Alderman (Adelaide) 1988–1990; Consultant Thomson Playford (Adelaide) 1995–1996; Member Bar Chambers 1997–2003; Hanson Chambers 2003–2006 Fellow of the Australian Academy of Law (FAAL)
Judge District Court SA 2006–2012
Justice Supreme Court since 2012

James David Edwardson QC

photo courtesy David Edwardson

born: 14 March 1961

educated: St Peters College Admitted: 1984
QC 2006

career: Bar Chambers since 1988; Executive Member of SA Bar Association; Chair Criminal Law Committee (SA Bar Association); Panel member of RAAF Legal Reserves (SQNLDR); Past member of Council of Law Society of SA; Past member of Criminal Lawyers' Committee (Law Society of SA)

Martin Gerard Hinton QC

photo supplied

born: 3 May 1965

educated: St Ignatius College, University of Adelaide LLB, BA (Jur), LLM; London School of Economics LLM; admitted: 1989
QC 2006

career: Solicitor-General SA 2008–2016, Adj Prof University of Adelaide Justice Supreme Court 2016–2019 Fellow Australian Academy of Law Director, Public Prosecutions (ODDP) SA since 2019
Publications include: co–editor *Indigenous Australians and the Law* (Rigney 1996 1st Ed; Taylor & Francis 2008 2nd Ed.); co–editor *Essays in Advocacy* (University of Adelaide Press 2012), co–editor *The Crown* (University of Adelaide Press, 2018)

Timothy Laurence Stanley QC

photo courtesy Tim Stanley

Son of: Brian and Noreen Stanley
born: 30 March 1959

educated: Rostrevor College, the University of Adelaide and the University of Western Australia
Admitted: 1982
QC 2006

career: Hanson Chambers 1989–2011
Justice Supreme Court since 2011

Michael Greig Evans QC

photo courtesy *The Advertiser*

born: 1 March 1959

Admitted: 1981
QC 2008

Career: Bar Chambers 1994–2004, Hanson Chambers 2004–2010, Crown Solicitor 2010–2016, Chief Judge, District Court SA since 2016

Simon Patrick O'Sullivan QC

photo courtesy Patrick O'Sullivan

Son of Group Captain Joseph Thaddeus O'Sullivan (ret'd) OBE, OAM and Zena Victoria Mary O'Sullivan
born: 21 January 1959

educated: St Ignatius College (1976), University of Adelaide (1981), Charles Sturt University (2002)
Admitted: 1981
QC 2008

career: Hong Kong AG Chambers 1988–1992, joined the independent bar 1997 Edmund Barton Chambers 1997–2018, Jeffcott Chambers 2018
President SABA 2012–2014, Vice President ABA 2015, President ABA 2016
Judge District Court SA since 2018

Married, 3 children recreation: Rugby Union, fly fishing, walking

James Peter Pearce QC

born: 28 February 1965

Admitted: 1988
QC 2008

career: Office of the Director of Public Prosecutions

Neville Grant Rochow QC

photo courtesy Neville Rochow

parents and occupations: Donald Edwin Rochow (Royal Australian Navy; marine surveyor and engineer) and Mavis Lillian Mason
born: 20 February 1956

educated: Enfield High School; University of Adelaide Law School (LLB Hons LLM PhD), Deakin University Law School (LLM)
Admitted: 1983
SC 2008 QC 2019

career: Judge's Associate: Zelling J and ACJ (researcher for Zelling J while he was chair of the then Law Reform Committee); Genders Wilson & Partners, Baker & McKenzie (Melbourne); University of Adelaide: Tutor in Evidence; Examiner in Criminal Procedure; Occasional lecturer; Associate Professor (Adjunct); Notre Dame: Professor (Adjunct); South Australian Bar Council; Federal Court
Liaison Committee; (the then) Trade Practices Committee; Convenor (with Professor David Round) of the national Competition Law & Economics Workshop, now the Uni SA and ACCC Competition Law and Economics Workshop; Co–Founder of Howard Zelling Chambers; Government Relations Adviser at the European Union in Brussels, Belgium
Languages: German and French

Married to Penelope Anne Edwards
Naval & Military Club

Michael James Roder QC

photo courtesy Michael Roder

son of John Herbert Roder (solicitor and judge, DCSA) and Denise Charlotte Roder (scientist and lecturer SA College of Advanced Education)
born: 2 January 1963

educated: St Peter's College 1975–1979, University of Adelaide (LLB Hons 1980–1984), GDLP 1985
admitted: 1985
SC 2008 QC 2019

career: Nicholls Gervasi 1986–1989; Norman Waterhouse 1989–2003; independent bar 2003; Howard Zelling Chambers since March 2003

married: Gilda 2d
recreation: Kooyonga Golf Club

Ian Carlyle Robertson SC

photo courtesy Will Russell

Son of: Walter Ian (chartered accountant) and Ann Thelma (secretary)
born: 2 August 1962

educated: St. Ignatius College, University of Adelaide, SAIT
Admitted: 1986
SC 2008

career: Jeffcott Chambers; Advocacy Training Council (ABA), 2008, Chair 2016; Australian Advocacy Institute Ltd (director); International Advocacy Training Council (Consultant) 2016; SA Bar Association Council 1998–2008, 2010–, President 2016–2018

Martin Andrew Frayne SC

photo courtesy JC

born: 18 April 1955

admitted: 1978
SC 2009

career: Jeffcott Chambers since 1987.

Simon Frederick Stretton SC

photo courtesy Simon Stretton

Son of: Professor Hugh Stretton AC and Jenifer Stretton
born: 23 December 1955

admitted: 1979
SC 2009

career: associate Hon Justice Dame Roma Mitchell AC QC 1980; joined independent bar 1982; Wellington Chambers, Market Street Chambers, Mitchell Chambers; Captain, The Australian Debating Team 1987–1989; General Counsel, NSW Crime Commission 1990; General Counsel, NSW ICAC 1992; Commissioner Australian Securities Commission 1995; Residential Tenancies Tribunal 1999; Adjunct Professor of law 2009, UniSA; Companies Auditors and Liquidators Disciplinary Board (Cwlth) 2004; Secretary, SA Bar Association 2003; Legal Committee of the Corporations and markets Advisory Committee (Cwlth) 2005; Crown Solicitor SA 2005–2010 Judge District Court SA since 2010

recreation: North Adelaide Football Club, music

Stuart William Henry QC

photo courtesy Stuart Henry

Parents: William Nelson Henry and Janetta Alexander Henry. Both self employed.
born: 24 August 1959
educated: Henley High School, University of Adelaide (LLB 1980), GDLP 1981; admitted: 1981
SC 2009 QC 2019

career: Assoc. Justice Sangster 1982, SA Police 1983; Mellor Gardner Beamond and Page 1980s; Ward and Partners 1980s–1990s; Carrington Chambers. Past member and president of the SA Division of the National Environmental Law Association

Married: Fiona 3 children. Recreation: Grange Golf Club, Cruising Yacht Club of South Australia

Hugh Anthony Lempriere Abbott SC

photo courtesy Hugh Abbott

Son of: Beverley Abbott, dentist, and Derek Athol Lempriere Abbott, solicitor, partner of Lempriere Abbott McLeod with his brother Charles Anthony Lempriere Abbott, solicitor, sons of Justice Charles Arthur Hillas Lempriere Abbott
born: 23 March 1960

educated: St Peter's College, University of Adelaide. Admitted: 1983
SC 2009

career: Jeffcott Chambers since 1999; Law Society Committee on the Justice Ipp Reforms to the Law of Negligence; Law Society Ethics and Practice Committee.

Married. Adelaide University Football Club, Adelaide University Cricket Club, Royal Adelaide Golf Club, yoga, body surfing, walking, music, flamenco, reading

Grant Raymond Algie QC

photo courtesy Grant Algie

Son of: Brian (stoker, shearer, steel fixer, farmer) and Beryl (usherette, model, homemaker)
born: 1960 Edithburgh SA

educated: Yorketown Area School, Immanuel College, University of Adelaide (LLB) GDLP admitted: 1983 SC 2009 QC 2019

career: general practice Whyalla 1983, Mitchell Chambers (foundation member), Elliott Johnston Chambers from 2017

current custodian of the full bottom wig commissioned for Sir Harry Alderman KC in 1943

William Penn Boucaut QC

photo courtesy Len King Chambers

Son of: James Penn Boucaut (solicitor) and Constance Stephens Boucaut
born: 29 July 1951

educated: Prince Alfred College, University of Adelaide Admitted: 1975 SC 2010 QC 2019

career: Edmund Barton Chambers, Len King Chambers

married: Lindsey 3 children

Gregory Peter Gerard Mead SC

photo courtesy Greg Mead

born: 12 August 1956

educated: Blackfriars Priory School, University of Adelaide (LLB 1978)
admitted: 1980
SC 2010

career: Herriman, McEvoy and Gilchrist (1979–1986); Legal Services Commission of SA since 1986; Manager of the LSC Criminal Law Practice 1991–2005; Chief Counsel, Legal Services Commission since 2005

David Michael Berman SC

born: 29 June 1955

Admitted: 1982
SC 2010

career: Campbell Chambers 1995–2013
Justice Family Court since 2013

Paul Francis Muscat SC

photo courtesy Paul Muscat

Son of: Paul (labourer) and Margaret (nurse aide)
born: 1 October 1962

educated: St Michael's College (1979), University of of Adelaide (LLB) (1984), Graduate Diploma in Legal Practice (1985) admitted: 1984
SC 2010

career: Career: Solicitor at Camatta Lempens (Port Adelaide) (1985–1993); Prosecutor at the Office of the Director of Public Prosecutions (State) (1994–2005); Head of the Criminal Law Division at the Legal Services Commission (2006–2012); Bowden–Brompton Community Legal Service Board member (1985–1990); Parks Community after hours Legal Advisory Service (1985–1989); Duty Solicitor Service Port Adelaide Magistrates Court (1985–1993); Law Society Criminal Law Committee (1986–2012); National Legal Aid Criminal Law Committee (2006–2012) Criminal Justice Ministerial Taskforce (SA) (2006–2011); Legal Services Commission Review Committee (2011–2012)
Judge District Court SA since 2012

married 2d

Liesl Jane Chapman SC

photo courtesy Len King Chambers

born: 18 June 1970
Admitted: 1993
SC 2010

career: Edmund Barton Chambers 2005–2007, Jeffcott Chambers 2007–2012, Len King Chambers 2012–2017
Judge District Court since 2017

Adam Patrick Kimber SC

photo courtesy Edmund Barton Chambers

born: 30 September 1969

admitted: 1993
SC 2010

career: Assoc Chief Justice Len King 1994–1995 Wallmans Director, Public Prosecutions (ODDP) SA 2012–2019, Edmund Barton Chambers 2019–2020
Judge District Court since 2020

recreation: Adelaide University Cricket Club

Geraldine Davison SC

born: 18 June 1962
educated: Admitted: 1986
SC 2011

Judge District Court since 2012

Andrew Leonard Tokley QC

photo courtesy Andrew Tokley

Son of: Albert and Hilda Tokley (dec.)
born: 6 January 1959

educated: LLB (Hons) BA University of Adelaide; admitted: 1983
SC 2012 QC 2019

career: joined independent bar 1997 Torrens Chambers 1997–2008, Anthony Mason Chambers 2008–, 5 Wentworth (Sydney) 2010–

Sandra McDonald SC

born: 24 June 1969

Admitted: 1993
SC 2012

Acting Director of Public Prosecutions

Dr Christopher David Bleby SC

photo courtesy Christopher Bleby

Son of: Hon. David John Bleby QC (barrister and justice, Supreme Court SA) and Elizabeth Mary Bleby (social worker)
born: 12 December 1969

educated: Pulteney Grammar School, Mita National High School, Tokyo; University of Adelaide BA (Hons), LLB (Hons); University of South Australia (GCLP); University of Cambridge (PhD) admitted: 1995
SC 2012

career: Assoc Justice John Perry 1996; ODPP (Public Prosecutions), Attorney-General's Dept (Policy and Research) and Crown Solicitor's Office 1996–1997; Crown Solicitor's Office 2000–2004; Hanson Chambers 2004–2014; Crown Advocate SA 2014–2016; Solicitor-General SA 2016–2020; Justice Supreme Court SA and Court of Appeal since 4 May 2020;
Fellow of the Australian Academy of Law

married: Meg Bleby 3d
recreation: cycling, drawing, painting

Thomas Patrick Duggan QC

photo courtesy Bar Chambers

born: 14 April 1972

Admitted: 1996
SC 2012 QC 2019

career: Edmund Barton Chambers 2004–2012, Bar Chambers since 2012

Samuel John Doyle SC

photo courtesy Samuel Doyle

Son of: Marie Doyle (social worker and student counsellor) and the Hon. John Doyle AC QC, Chief Justice 1995–2012
born: 15 March 1973

educated: St. Ignatius' College Adelaide University (BCom & LLB (Hons) Oxford University (BCL)
admitted: 1998
SC 2012

career: Assoc Justice Bruce Lander 1996 Tutor Equity, University of Adelaide Jeffcott Chambers 2002–2015
Justice Supreme Court SA since 2015

married with 4d

Thomas William Cox QC

photo courtesy Tom Cox

son of Brian Cox (lawyer) and Anna Cox
born: 13 July 1970

educated: Prince Alfred College, University of Adelaide (B.A. Hons, LL.B. Hons 1993), Columbia University, New York (LL.M 1997)
Admitted: 1994
SC 2013 QC 2019

career: Office of the Director of Public Prosecutions (SA) 1994–1996; Cleary, Gottlieb, Steen & Hamilton, New York (1997–2001, 2004) & Brussels (2002–2003), joined the independent bar 2005, member of Hanson Chambers since 2011

Married with 4 children. Recreation: reading, travel, films / TV, spectator at performing arts, football & cricket

Mark Andrew Norman SC

born: 17 October 1963

educated: BA (Hons) from the University of London, Diploma in Law from the University of Westminster; admitted to practice at the Bar of England and Wales, 1989; admitted NSW and SA: 2006
SC 2013

career: Office of the Director of Public Prosecutions (ODPP) SA since 2005

Claire Mary O'Connor SC

photo courtesy Claire O'Connor

born: 19 October 1958

educated: St Philomena's College and Otago University, Dunedin, New Zealand Admitted: New Zealand 1980 South Australia 1982
SC 2014

career: Australian Advocacy Association and Adelaide University (past); Law Society of South Australia; former member of various sub–committees including Diversity; former member of Law Council Diversity Committee. Former member of the Occupational Therapists Board; former member and former chair person of the Women's Legal Service; former member of the Refugee Advocacy Service (SA); member and current chair of the SA Council for Civil Liberties; Aboriginal Deaths in Custody, Kapunda Road Royal Commission, Hindmarsh Island Royal Commission; SA Bar Association. Villeneuve Smith Chambers, Accredited Mediator since 2019 Awards: The Australian Lawyers Alliance Human Rights award, the Law Society of SA Brian Withers award for services to the profession, the SA Law Society Bulletin Article of the Year award, the Law Society Justice Award

2 children 2 grandchildren
recreation/interests: cycling, long distance hiking, human rights

Ian Douglas Press SC

born: 27 March 1963

educated: University of Adelaide,
admitted: 1989
SC 2014

career: Legal Services Commission
Office of Public Prosecutions (ODDP)
SA
Judge District Court SA since 2020

Darren John Blight QC

photo courtesy Darren Blight

Parents: John Francis Blight (farmer and grazier), Leone Veril Blight (school teacher)
born: 2 June 1973

educated: Tintinara Area School; Marryatville High School; University of Adelaide
admitted: 1995
SC 2014 QC 2019

career: Ward & Partners 1995–2002, Piper Alderman 2002–2004, Edmund Barton Chambers 2005–2013, Hanson Chambers 2014–2020, Nexus Chambers since 2020 (founding member)

Married 3 daughters

Brendon Charles Roberts QC

photo courtesy Bar Chambers

born: 20 July 1972

admitted: 1995
SC 2014 QC 2019

career: joined independent bar 2008,
Bar Chambers since 2008

Charles Samuel (Sam) Lempriere Abbott QC

photo courtesy Sam Abbott

parents: Charles Anthony Lempriere Abbott, solicitor and Judith Millroy Abbott
born: 5 March 1971

educated: St Peters College (1988) and University of Adelaide (BA, LLB(Hons) 1995)
admitted: 1996
SC 2014, QC 2019

career: Associate to Justice Brian Cox 1996; WGCDR, RAAF Specialist Reserve; Bar Chambers since 2004

married: 3 children recreation: soccer, golf, tennis

Sophie Victoria David SC

photo courtesy Sophie David

born: 7 July 1971

educated: Firbank Grammar School, Brighton, Victoria 1986–1988, Australian National University 1989–1995 BA/LLB
admitted: 1996
SC 2014

career: Legal Services Commission, SA 1996–1998; Director of Public Prosecutions, SA 1998–2003; joined independent bar 2003, Edmund Barton Chambers 2003–2009; Bar Chambers 2010–2015

Appointed Judge District Court SA December 2015

The Hon. John Robert Rau SC

photo courtesy John Rau

born: 20 March 1959

educated: Henley High School, University of Adelaide LLB 1980, GDLP 1981 admitted: 1981
SC 2016

career: Duncan Groom Carabelas & Hannon 1982–1985; Hawke Government advisor 1985–1988; Johnston Withers 1988–1997; joined independent bar 1997, Murray Chambers 1998–2010; since 2018

Attorney-General Labor SA 2010–2018
various SA ministerial portfolios 2010–2018
Deputy Premier 2011–2018

Graham Donald Edmonds-Wilson QC

photo courtesy Graham Edmonds-Wilson

born: 2 April 1963

educated: LLB (Hons) 1986, B Ec 1987, LLM 2000 admitted: 1987 SC 2016 QC 2019

career: Baker McEwin and successor firms Baker O'Loughlin and Minter Ellison 1988–2007; Partner, Minter Ellison 1998–2007; joined the SA Bar 2007, Howard Zelling Chambers since 2007.

married: Ellen Edmonds-Wilson; 1d

Scott Grant Henchliffe QC

photo courtesy Scott Henchliffe

Son of: Derek Frank Henchliffe (bank manager) and Judith Anne Henchliffe (legal secretary)
born: 28 February 1969

educated: Norwood High School, University of Adelaide (B, Ec., LLB, LLM)
admitted: 1991
SC 2016 QC 2019

career: joined independent bar 2004; Edmund Barton Chambers since 2005; co–editor *Criminal Law SA* since 2019

recreation: Kooyonga Golf Club

Emily Telfer SC

photo courtesy Len King Chambers

born: 29 March 1973

educated: Marryatville High School, South Australia
admitted: 1996
SC 2016

career: Assoc. to the Hon. Justice Nyland, Supreme Court SA 1997. Public Prosecutions (ODPP) SA; Counsel Assisting, Child Protection Systems Royal Commission 2014–2016. Member and Public Officer, Australian and New Zealand Association for Psychology, Psychiatry and the Law (SA). Len King Chambers 2020–

Simon David Ower QC

photo courtesy Simon Ower

Son of: David and Gloria
born: 21 June 1976

educated: Le Fevre High School, Golden Grove High School, University of Adelaide (BA(Jur), LLB(Hons))
admitted: 2001
SC 2016 QC 2019

career: Assoc. to the Hon. Justice Sackville, Federal Court of Australia (2000–2001); Barrister, Edmund Barton Chambers (2002–2017) and Jeffcott Chambers since 2018.
appointments: Legal Practitioners Disciplinary Tribunal 2018– (Deputy Presiding Member, 2020–)

married: Amanda, 3 children (2 s 1 d)

Michael Jonathan Wait SC

photo courtesy Attorney-General's Dept

Son of Robert Noel Wait (lecturer in history and design) and Rosemary Clare Wait (history teacher)
born: 19 April 1973

educated: University of Adelaide (Arts Hons, LLB Hons); Cambridge University (LLM Hons)
admitted: 2003
SC 2016

career: Assoc. to Justice Rodney Madgwick, Federal Court of Australia (1999–2000); Assoc. to Justice Mary Gaudron, High Court of Australia (2001); Crown Solicitor's Office (2004–2017); Tutor (p/time) in Constitutional Law, Administrative Law, Evidence and Advocacy, and Government Contracts at University of Adelaide (2004–2014); Australian Association of Constitutional Law (2004–present); Australian Institute of Administrative Law (2004–present)
Crown Solicitor and Crown Advocate 2017–2020
Solicitor–General from 2020 (August)

Married to Pierina Reina, 2 children

Michael Robert Burnett QC

born: 8 April 1959

admitted: 1981
SC 2018

career: Bar Chambers 2003–2020
Judge District Court SA since 2020

Alan John Lindsay SC

photo courtesy Alan Lindsay

Son of Grahame Lindsay (Surveyor General) and Glenys Lindsay
born: 18 July 1959

educated: Blackwood High School, Nightcliff High School and University of Adelaide (LLB Hons); GDLP
admitted: 1982
SC 2018

career: Employed at Poveys, partner in Cridlands, joined independent bar 2007, Wright Chambers and Jeffcott Chambers; Co–founder Aboriginal Law Students Mentoring Program; Law Society Justice Award 2018

Spouse: Alison Lowrie, 2 children

Domenico Petraccaro SC

photo courtesy Domenico Petraccaro

born: 11 August 1961

educated: University of Adelaide 1987–1990 BA (Hons); 1990–1993 LLB (Hons)
admitted: 1994
SC 2018

career: Judge's Associate (Justice BR Cox 1995); Caldicott & Co Lawyers (1996–1999); Legal Services Commission (1999–2000); Commonwealth Director of Public Prosecutions (2000–2002); Office of the Director of Public Prosecutions (SA) (2002–current)

Dr Rachael Frances Gray QC

photo courtesy Rachael Gray

born: 7 August 1971

educated: University of Adelaide BA 1992, LLB (Hons 1995), Zelling–Gray Scholarship, PhD 2007; Bonython Prize 2008
admitted: 1995
SC 2018 QC 2019

career: Assoc Justice Prior 1996; Crown Solicitor's Office, Counsel Assisting the State Coroner and Deputy State Coroner; joined independent bar 2009, Howard Zelling Chambers; founder Victoria Square Chambers 2015. Author of *The Constitutional Jurisprudence and Judicial Method of the High Court of Australia: the Dixon, Mason and Gleeson Eras*, Adelaide, Presidian, 2008.

Single 3 children

Heath David Barklay QC

photo courtesy Heath Barklay

born: 31 January 1975

educated: Bond University 1994–1996
Admitted: 1997
SC 2018 QC 2019

career: Mangan Ey & Assoc 1998–2003; Crown Prosecutor SA 2003–2005 and 2007–2010; Public Defender's Office Solomon Islands 2005–2007; joined independent bar 2010; Co–founder of Len King Chambers, Edmund Barton Chambers since 2013

married: 3 children

Endnotes

1 W B Fisse and D St.L Kelly. "Political influence in the appointment of Queen's Counsel ", *Australian Law Journal* 44 ALJ 318 at 326.

Conclusion

South Australia's independent bar may have been a "reluctant debutante" in its beginnings but it continues to prosper and expand. The bar now numbers around 225 members, roughly 25% larger than in 2006.

Back then I suggested three questions that could be asked about its future direction: 1) will it continue to organise itself in small sets of chambers according to the model set by Bar Chambers? 2) will it ever seek to become a "separate" bar like those in England and in New South Wales and Queensland? and 3) will the proportion of women barristers continue to increase?

In response to the first question, it has remained an obvious yes. In relation to also setting up in an old bluestone building, less so. The trend has been for newer chambers to lease floors in multistorey buildings rather than buy free-standing old buildings. The older established chambers such as Bar, Hanson, Jeffcott and Edmund Barton have remained in historical buildings, even when moving as in the case of Jeffcott, and also Anthony Mason, which began as Divett Chambers. The long-vacant site next to the courts on Gouger Street fifteen years ago finally was built on, and the latest chambers, Nexus, has set up there. Their vision is a move away from the historic sensibility of the Inns of Court to the immediate priority of being as close as possible to the courts and ability to adapt inner design more easily to future needs.

In regards to a formal separation of solicitors and barristers in the South Australian legal profession, that appears to have faded. The current admission as both continues to prove its value in a relatively small jurisdiction where barristers and solicitors can quickly switch if needs be. The strength of the South Australian independent bar also remains that so many of its members have experience in solicitor work.

On the proportion of women barristers continuing to increase, social forces on the way families are organised remain the great obstacle. The proportion of female barristers as we noted earlier in the book, remains around 20%, a figure that appears more or less the general percentage across common law jurisdictions anywhere. That would suggest that for women, South Australia's independent bar is not peculiar in comparison with the other Australian States, New Zealand, or the United Kingdom. In other words, no better, no worse.

We are happily far from the days when women were not even permitted to practise by law. From Henry VIII until the mid-nineteenth century even non-Anglican men in England were prevented from joining the bar. In South Australia, Roman Catholic men were not appointed permanently to the Supreme Court all the way until 1959 with James Brazel. Don Dunstan's appointment of Roma Mitchell in 1965 smashed the double discrimination across Australia. A little too slowly perhaps, society has been learning that a prerequisite to being a skilled barrister is ability and experience, not gender nor being a member of a particular social class or religion.

From 2020 the future of the South Australian independent bar is going to depend more than ever, perhaps, on the impact of technology, especially the ever-increasing speed of digital document exchange, the improving accessibility and searchability of authorities, of increasing video appearances in court. A barrister needs less to have leather-bound reports lining their chambers walls than a reliable and speedy internet connection. The courts are able to accept electronic submissions. Covid has given everything a huge kick and at the time of writing, many barristers remain working mostly from home. Long-formed habits of generations have irreversibly changed. Such shifts will improve the flexibility for those who are mothers, and who knows, set new directions for the whole profession.

Bibliography

Abel, Richard L. *The Legal Profession in England and Wales*. Oxford: Blackwell, 1988.

Abel, Richard L. *American Lawyers*. Oxford: Oxford University Press, 1989.

Abel-Smith, Brian & Stevens, Robert. *Lawyers and the Courts*. London: Heinemann, 1967.

Bennett, J. M. *History of the New South Wales Bar*. Sydney: Law Book Co., 1969.

Bennett, J.M. *Sir Francis Forbes*. Leichardt (NSW), Federation Press, 2001.

Cassidy, J. A. & Corkery, J. F. *Aldermans Barristers and Solicitors*. Adelaide: Aldermans, 1988.

Cockburn, Stewart. *Playford : Benevolent Despot*. Kent Town (Sth. Aus.): Axiom, 1991.

Dean, Arthur. *A Multitude of Counsellors: A History of the Bar of Victoria*. Melbourne: F. W. Cheshire, 1968.

Disney, Julian et al. *Lawyers*. Sydney: The Law Book Company, 1977.

Forbes, J.R.S. *The Divided Legal Profession in Australia*. Sydney: The Law Book Company, 1979.

Forde, John Leonard. *The Story of the Bar of Victoria, 1839-1891*. Melbourne: Whitcombe & Tombs, no date.

Hague, Ralph. *Hague's History of the Law in South Australia, 1837-1867*. Adelaide: University of Adelaide Barr Smith Press, 2005.

Holdsworth, Sir William. *A History of English Law*. London: Methuen and Sweet & Maxwell, 1966. Seventh Edition.

Johnston, Ross. *History of the Queensland Bar*. Brisbane: Bar Association of Queensland, ca. 1978.

Kelly, Bernard W. A *Short History of the English Bar*. London: Geo. Allen & Co., 1908.

Parry, Edward Abbott. *The Seven Lamps of Advocacy*. London: Fisher Unwin, 1923.

Preiss, Ken & Oborn, Pamela. *The Torrens Park Estate*. Adelaide: Published by the authors, 1991.

Prest, Wifrid R. *The Inns of Court under Elizabeth I and the Early Stuarts*. London: Longman, 1972.

Prest, Wilfrid (ed.) . *Lawyers in Early Modern Europe and America*. London: Croon Helm, 1981.

Prest, Wilfrid R. *The Rise of the Barristers*. Oxford: Clarendon Press, 1986.

Rubin, G. R. & Sugarman, David (eds.) *Law, Economy and Society, 1750-1914: Essays in the History of English Law*. Abington (Oxon.): Professional Books, 1984.

Sawyer, Geoffrey. "Division of a Fused Legal Profession: The Australasian Experience" (1966) 16 U. Tor. L.J. 245.

Vroland, R. N. "Organisation of the Legal Profession in Australia". G. Paton (ed.). The Commonwealth of Australia: The Development of its Laws and Constitution. 1952.

Periodicals

Australian Bar Gazette. Sydney: The Law Book Co., 1964-1970.

Australian Bar Review. Sydney: Butterworths, 1985-.

Australian Law Journal. Sydney: The Law Book Co., Vol. 27, No. 3, July 30, 1953. "The Eighth Legal Convention of the Law Council of Australia", pp. 133-224.

Law Calendar. South Australian Attorney-General's Department. Adelaide: Government Printer, 1889-.

South Australian Year Book. Adelaide: Commonwealth Bureau of Statistics, South Australian Office, 1966-. (Formerly Official Year Book of South

Australia)

Articles

Brennan, the Hon. Sir Gerald. "Why be a Judge?" (1996) 14 Aust Bar Rev 89.

W B Fisse and D St.L Kelly. "Political influence in the appointment of Queen's Counsel ", *Australian Law Journal* 44 ALJ 318 at 326.

Hart, Justice G. & Helman, John. "The Founding of the Australian Bar Association". *The Australian Bar Gazette*. Vol. 2, October 1968, pp. 3-7.

Mason, the Hon. Sir Anthony. "The Independence of the Bench; the Independence of the Bar and the Bar's Role in the Judicial System". (1993) 10 Aust Bar Rev 1.

Mildren, the Hon. Justice Dean. "A Short History of the Bar in the Northern Territory." (2001) 21 Aust Bar Rev 81.

Wells, W. A. N. "Examination in Chief." *Bulletin*. January, 1977, pp. 2-15.

2006 Edition Interviews

Michael Abbott QC
The Hon. Tim Anderson QC
Michael Barnett QC
Gordon Barrett QC
Michael Birchall
Anthony Bishop
The Hon. David Bleby QC
Kevin Borick QC
Geoffrey Britton
Gabby Brown
Tim Bryant
Rob Cameron
Pam Cleland

Professor Michael Detmold
The Hon. John Doyle AC QC
The Hon. John von Doussa AC QC
Mr John Firth
Ms Joana Fuller (now Her Hon. Judge)
The Hon. Tom Gray QC
Mr Geoffrey Hackett-Jones QC
Mr David Haines QC
Mr Andrew Harris QC
Mr Brian Hayes QC
Mr Paul Heywood-Smith QC
The Hon. Sam Jacobs QC
Mrs Kate Jennings
The Hon. Elliott Johnston AO QC
Mr Andrew Jordan
Ms Margaret Kelly
The Hon. Len King AC QC
Robyn Layton AO QC
The Hon. Christopher Legoe AO QC
Ms Holly Leeson
Mr Stuart Lindsay
Mr David Lovell QC
Mr Neil Lowrie
The Hon. Robin Millhouse QC
The Hon. Justice Steven Millsteed
The Hon. Robert Mohr
The Hon. Ted Mullighan QC
Ms Frances Nelson QC
Mr Peter Norman OAM
The Hon. Justice Margaret Nyland AM
The Hon. John Perry AO QC
Mr Mark Pickhaver
Ms Lindy Powell QC
Mr Kelvyn Prescott CSM
Mr Neville Rochow QC
Mr Anthony Russell QC
Ms Marie Shaw QC
Ms Shane Spence
The Hon. John Sulan QC
Mr Sydney Tilmouth QC
Ms Vickianne West
The Hon. Tim Williams QC
Mr Andrew Wilson

Index of People and Chambers

This index covers as many people and chambers as possible, but does not claim to be exhaustive. Some names in photo captions may not be included.

A

Jane Abbey 131, 132
Wendy Abraham 198
Charles (Arthur Hillas Lempriere) Abbott 11
Charles (Sam) Abbott 55, 257
Hugh Abbott 68, 106, 108, 237
Michael Abbott vii, 55, 76, 77, 107, 163
Philip Adams 92
Grant Algie vii, 106, 108, 126, 127, 238
Gilbert Aitken 106
Peter Allan 182
Anthony Allen 131, 132
Christopher Allen 131, 132
Barry Amey 122
Martin Anders 87
Mark Anderson 84, 102, 109, 124
Timothy (Tim) Anderson 23, 61, 62, 64, 66, 173, 275
Andrew Jordan 78, 121, 276
R B Andrews 7
David Angel 23, 53, 155
Anthony Mason Chambers 109
Stephen Apps 54, 58, 87, 90
Stephen Archer 33
Ben Armstrong 88
Thomas Arnold 5
J F Astley 146, 150
Athol Olsson 201
Brian Austin 97, 100
Australian Bar Association 3, 15, 16, 19, 21, 35, 41, 44, 172

B

Francis Bacon 141
Joshua Baden Teague 55
J H Bagot 11
Andrew Baillie 55
Brian Baillie 79, 82
Adam Baker 55
Sir Richard Baker 98
Baker McEwin Millhouse & Co. 14
Bar Association of Queensland 16
Bar Chambers 19, 21, 23, 24, 48, 49, 52, 53, 55, 56, 57, 58, 98, 153, 155, 114, 147, 151, 152, 60, 162, 163, 185, 187, 195, 206
Heath Barklay 88, 90, 131, 269
Anne Barnett 68, 73, 113
Michael Barnett vii, 68, 73, 113, 275
Peter Barnes 92
Michelle Barnes vii, 131, 132
Gordon Barrett viii, 48, 76, 77, 106, 108, 191, 275
Bar Roll ix, 15, 27, 30, 42, 74, 75, 139, 140
Robert Barr Smith 10
Tom Elder Barr Smith 10
Patrick Barry 118
Edmund Barton 88
Miss E G Bartsch 21, 56
Jayne Basheer 84
Max Basheer 201
Josephine Battiste 107
Barry Beazley 86, 210
Maurice Bednall 10
Louise Bedson 102, 129
Michael Bell 82
Enzo Belperio 55
Eliza Bergin 110
Jeremy Bentham 5
David Berman 83, 85, 241
Anthony Besanko 25, 67, 73, 91, 93, 94, 73, 188
Tom Besanko 68
David Billington 118
Michael Birchall vii, 21, 48, 53, 58, 59, 275
Nicholas Birchall 53, 171

(James) Tom Birchall 109, 110, 112, 118
Lord Birkett 33
R A Blackburn 57
William Blackstone 6
Christopher Bleby 61, 64, 65, 248
David Bleby vii, 67, 69, 70, 73, 158, 275
Gordon (E H) Bleby 154, 158
Simon Blewett 134
Darren Blight vii, 62, 87, 135, 255
Malcolm Blue 54, 58, 206
Mark Blumberg 91, 95
David Blyth 109, 135
Mark Boehm 102
Derek (D W) Bollen 61, 62, 64, 146, 178, 199
Benjamin Boothby 7, 63
Kevin Borick vii, 23, 74, 78, 121, 202, 275
Audrey Bosboom 110
William (Bill) Boucaut 87, 90, 131, 132, 239
Liz Bowering 106
Joseph Bowler 129
Francis Boylan 53
Frank Boylan 22, 57
Michael Boylan 86, 90, 209
Melissa Boyle (née Perry) 129
William Braithwaite 77
Catherine Branson 54, 93, 185
John (Dr J J) Bray 11, 24, 57, 102, 103, 104, 103, 140, 153, 157, 162, 163 182, 205, 214, 218
J F Brazel 12, 13,149
Donald Brebner 10, 57, 155
Peter Brebner 214
David Bright 23, 54
Geoffrey Britton vii, 97, 98, 99, 100
Christopher Brohier 122, 123
Lord Brougham 6
Dean Brown 26, 69
Timothy Bryant 79, 80, 81, 82
Paul Bullock 68, 73, 109
Sally Burgess vii
Michael Burnett 55, 265
Brendan Burns 53
Francis Burt 15, 23, 47
Paul Bullock 68
Marie Beuzeville Byles 28

C

Rob (Robert) Cameron 23, 54, 58, 59
Lord John Campbell 84
Campbell Chambers 83
Thomas Carlyle 5
Roderick Chamberlain 9, 149
David Chapman 74, 86
Liesl Chapman 68, 87, 131, 243
Vickie Chapman 78, 109, 111, 121, 142, 143
Natalie Charlesworth 109, 133
David Childs 124
Steven Churches 126, 127
Cicero 4, 18
Kerry Clark 92
Gresley Clarkson 15, 16
Dean Clayton 42, 54, 58, 59, 186
Pam Cleland vii, 23, 27, 28, 49, 74, 75, 127
Cleland Chambers 23, 74, 202
Mark Clisby 79
Christopher Cocks 53, 77, 97, 98, 99, 100, 176
Judith Cocks 129
Stuart Cole 97, 98, 99, 100, 122, 123
Ian Colgrave 117
Andrew Collett 92, 134
Rosemary Colton 82
Mardi Conduit 88
Sir Charles Cooper 63
William Tomsey Cooper 55
Gary Coppola 78, 117
Jack Cornish 10
John Costello 91
Thomas (Tom) Cox 62, 251
Anthony Crocker 68, 73
David Crocker 80, 88, 90
Andrew Culshaw 131, 132
John Cummins 83
Paul Cuthbertson 86, 118, 88, 90, 215

D

Arturo Dal Cin 92, 117, 119
Candida D'Arcy 88, 90
Graham Dart 97, 100
Paul d'Assumpçao 118
Doreen Davey 218
John Davey 28
Rosemary Davey 86, 90
Michael David 53, 114, 168, 216, 113, 114, 168
Sophie David 87, 90, 258
Geraldine Davison 245
Sue Davies 23
Dianne Dawson 49
Paris Dean 133
Bruce Debelle 54, 159
Carrie Demertzis 113
Maria Demosthenous 110
Larissa Detmold 117
Michael Detmold 21, 53
Jo-anne Deuter 87, 109, 112
Diana Dibden 102, 104, 116
Charles Dickens 5, 84
Meredith Dickson vii, 78, 121, 124, 125
John Dillon 84, 126, 127
Divett Chambers (now Anthony Mason) 109
Stephen Dowd 79, 80
Benjamin (Ben) Doyle 61
John Doyle vii, 23, 38, 61, 62, 64, 66, 143, 156, 276
Samuel Doyle 68, 250
Mark Douglas 92
John von Doussa viii, 26, 54, 67, 69, 71, 72, 73, 147, 276
Julie von Doussa 61
Adele du Barry 102, 105
R M (Ross) Duffy 12, 164, 204
Kevin Duggan 24, 54, 151
Tom Duggan 55, 87, 90, 249
Don Dunstan 11, 57, 103
Anthony Durkin 87

E

Geoffrey Eames 61, 64, 66, 177
Edmund Barton Chambers 48, 86, 115, 118, 89, 88, 176, 180, 181, 197, 205, 209, 210, 215
Graham Edmonds-Wilson 117, 260
David Edwardson 54, 58, 59, 140, 225
Doris Egerton 27
Christine Eicke 56
Nicholas Eid 124
Sir Thomas Elder 10
Lord Eldon 5, 6
Elizabeth Evatt Chambers 124
Jack Elliott 3, 9, 13, 14, 18, 19, 21
Robert Fenwick Elliott 117
Elliott Johnston Chambers 126
English legal profession 3, 6
Equity Chambers 116
Peter Eriksen 91, 118, 93, 95, 94
Ada Evans 27
Michael Evans 54, 59, 61, 65, 82, 228
Richard Evans 91, 94, 95, 117
Scott Evans vii, 68, 73, 88, 135

F

David Fabbro 126, 127
Fazio de Fazio 106, 108
Tricia Fehlberg 72
John Firth 122, 123
Robert (Bob) Fisher 11, 57
Nicholas (Nick) Floreani 68, 87, 113
Christina Flourentzou 118
Francis Forbes 18, 32
Sir John Forbes 6
Andrew Fowler-Walker 131, 132
Barry Fox 116
Vasilios Fragos 113
Martin Frayne vii, 67, 73, 234
Dora Fuda 102
Joana Fuller vii, 54, 58, 276

G

Paul Gabrynowicz 79, 82,
Mrs Gaskell 5
Mary Gaudron 29
Lauren Gavranich 88
Genders Wilson and Bray 74
Lewis Gentry 110, 135
Grant Germein 97, 99, 100
Sibyl Gibbs 28
Daniella Di Girolamo 92

Carey Goodall 68
Charles Henry Goode 110
Gordon Gratton 214
Malcolm Gray 106, 108, 160
Rachael Gray vii, 117, 133, 268
Thomas (Tom) Gray vii, xii, 54, 58, 162
Peter Green 185
The "Green Paper" 33
David Greenwell 48, 115, 86, 115, 118, 88
Flos Greig 27
Katarina Grenfell 92
Mark Griffin 122, 123, 219
Mark Grogan 102
(Edward) Ted Guthrie 110, 135

H

Geoffrey Hackett-Jones 61, 166, 276
David Haines 23, 74, 115, 86, 115, 118, 88, 201
Richard Halliday 91, 94, 95
Michelle Hamlyn 92
Kris Handshin 55, 131
Sir Richard Hanson 8, 62
Hanson Chambers 23, 25, 26, 57, 61, 62, 63, 64, 65, 146, 156, 164, 170, 173, 177, 192
Simon Hanus 68
C T Hargrave 12
Russel Harms 109
Andrew Harris vii, 48, 67, 71, 73, 204
Haroon Hassan 55
Lesley Hastwell 102
Brian Hayes vii, 25, 91, 93, 94, 95, 167
Tim Heffernan 87
Sally Heidenriech 92
Peter Heinrich 84
Scott Henchliffe vii, 87, 90, 113, 261
Stuart Henry 236
Henry Heuzenroeder vii, 80, 92
Taruna Heuzenroeder 92
Gary Hevey 74, 83
Paul Heywood-Smith 109, 110, 112, 208
Julian Hicks 102, 104
Martin Hinton 226
Mark Hoffmann 55, 143, 220
Richard Hogan 102, 104
David Hogarth 12, 147, 186
Martin Hoile 54, 58, 59, 110
William Holdsworth 18, 141
Gregory Holland 102, 103
Elisa Holmes 117, 119, 120
Andrea Horvath 102
David Howard 97, 99, 100
Howard Zelling Chambers 117
Hugh Burton Chambers 129
Noelle Hurley 84, 88, 90
Tony Hurren 88
Jonathon Hyde 86

I

John Ibbotson 113
Aileen Constance Ingleby 27
Rupert Ingleby 28

J

Timothy Jackson 79
Chad Jacobi 88
Samuel Jacobs 11, 57
Alison James 106
Helena Jasinski 91, 80, 82, 81, 95
Sir John Jeffcott 6, 69
Jeffcott Chambers 25, 26, 149, 67, 69, 71, 73, 147, 158, 73, 169, 172, 188, 203, 211
Catherine Jeffries 83
Barry Jenner 86
Kate Jennings 26, 49, 71
John Bray Chambers 102
Elliott Johnston 23, 29, 141, 182, 208
Edward Jolly vii, 83, 87, 90, 131, 132
Andrew Jones 80
Andrew Jordan 78, 121, 276

K

Robert Kane 107, 113
Penelope Kari 68, 84
J R Kearnan 11, 149, 174, 175
John Keen 79, 81, 82
Martin Keith 97, 99, 100, 117, 119
John Kelly 170
Margaret Kelly 122, 123
Patricia Kelly 212
Tim Kentish 92

Naomi Kereru 69
Adam Kimber 88, 244
Greg King 87
Len King 9, 11, 24, 26, 57, 34, 36, 37, 38, 40, 41, 44, 44
Charles Cameron Kingston 98
Kingston Chambers 97
Mary Kitson 27, 28
Patricia Knutson 74
Christopher Kourakis vii, 86, 143, 197
Bernard Krupka 68
Chris Kummerow 88

L

Bruce Lander 67, 72, 73, 169, 250
Simon Lane 54, 58, 59
Grahame Lang 113
Leanne Larosa 107
Law Council of Australia 16, 41, 158, 170
Law Society 24, 27, 32, 35, 39, 40, , 139, 94, 140, 146, 147, 153, 157, 44, 170, 179, 180, 181, 183, 184, 186, 187, 188, 197
Robert Lawson 67, 72, 73, 172
Robyn Layton vii, 29, 91, 95, 184
Alex Lazarevich 109
Ian Leckie 167
Vanessa Lee 102
Holly Leeson vii, 102, 129
Christopher Legoe 3, 9, 10, 11, 13, 14, 47, 53, 56, 113, 114, 125, 190
Legoe Chambers 113
Len King Chambers 131
Ron Levy 134
Taanya Lewis 125, 125
Libra Chambers 23, 74
Sir George Ligertwood 11
Craig Lind 107
Leonard (Len) Lindon 26, 67
Alan Lindsay 68, 266
Stuart Lindsay 78, 83, 118, 121
Patrick Liptak 102
Mark Livesey 55, 87, 221
Graham Loughlin 18, 98, 139
David Lovell vii, 67, 211
Neil Lowrie 25, 26, 67, 69, 70, 71, 73
Robert Lunn 161
Helen Luu 55
John Lyons 76, 106, 108

M

Arlene MacDonald 86
Heather Mack 122, 123
Marissa Mackie 110
Suzanne Mackenzie 55
Michael Magarey 117, 119
Sashi Maharaj 31, 91, 223
Adrian Maik 126, 127
Matoula Makris 110
Michael Manetta 68, 87, 109
John Mangan 165
Alexander Manos 117
John Mansfield 61, 62, 64, 66, 133, 170
Elizabeth Mansfield 126, 126
James Marcus 131, 132
Market Street Chambers 48, 77, 98, 107, 163, 191
Andrew Martin 23, 53, 59
Brian Martin 91, 95, 165
Clara Brett Martin 27
Rod Matheson 11, 57
Lord Maugham 33
Ross Mayne 77, 106
Sir Herbert Mayo 11
Craig McCarthy 83
Kenneth McCarthy 148
Brad McCloud 88
Sandra McDonald 247
Stephen McDonald 61
Samuel McDonough 131, 132
Stephen McEwen 122, 123, 222
John McGinn 129
James McMillan 92
Philip McNamara 83, 91, 95, 207
Brian McQuade 83
Terence McRae 97, 99, 100
Sir Edward McTiernan 151
Christine Mead 83, 85
Gregory Mead 240
Matthew Mead 113
William (Will) Mellor 135
Richard Mellows 79, 81, 82
Simon Milazzo 91, 95
David Miles 41

John Stuart Mill 5
Jane Miller 124
Robin Millhouse 3, 14, 21, 24, 53, 57, 152
Vivian (V R) Millhouse 11, 14, 152
Michael Mills 87
Steven Millsteed 55, 195
Stephen Mitchell vii, 109
Roma Mitchell 28, 74, 75, 108, 107, 187
Mitchell Chambers 48, 49, 76, 106, 160, 130, 191
Andrew Moffa 79, 83
Robert Mohr 21, 22, 53, 56, 57
Kristie Molloy 113
Simon Moncrieff 116
John Morcombe 83, 85
Neville Morcombe viii, 83, 87, 85, 87, 90, 180
Carrie Morrison 27
Peter Morrison 131
John Mortimer 26, 71
Geoffrey Muecke 67, 73
Edward (Ted) Mullighan 67, 149
Christian Munt 88
Rupert Murdoch 13, 15, 32
Matt Murphy 110
Murray & Cudmore 10
Sir George John Robert Murray 93
Murray Chambers 91, 93, 94, 95, 96, 165, 94, 167, 184, 188, 203, 207
Paul Muscat 242

N

R M (Bob) Napier 166
Sir Mellis Napier 11, 24, 57, 103, 140, 150, 157, 202
Joe Nelligan 9, 11, 18
Frances Nelson 29, 56, 78, 102, 103, 121, 140, 157
Paris Nesbit 98
D R Newman 11, 12
Nexus Chambers 49, 135, 136
Nicholas Niarchos 126, 127, 128
Kevin Nicholson 55, 61, 65, 224
Frederick William Niesche 56
Geoffrey Noble 23, 83, 84
Michael Noblet 53
Norman Waterhouse Mutton 10
Mark Norman 252
Helena Normanton 27
Margaret Nyland 23, 28, 74

O

Bernard O'Brien 82
Claire O'Connor 109, 253
Susan O'Connor 77
Dan O'Gorman 134
Damian O'Leary 55, 118
Mark O'Loughlin 87
Graham Olsson 179
(Simon) Patrick O'Sullivan 68, 72, 86, 90, 229
Robert Owen 5
Simon Ower 68, 87, 90, 263

P

Debbie De Palma 118
E W Palmer 12
Marita Pangallo 88, 118
Alex Panousakis 126, 127
Robert Park 83, 84
James Pearce 230
David Peek 67, 91, 95, 73, 203
John (J W) Perry viii, 24, 37, 44, 38, 54, 153, 156, 170, 187, 217, 248, 276
Melissa Perry 30, 44, 54, 58, 59, 217
Helen Pertsinidis 126
Domenico Petraccaro 267
A L Pickering 11, 12
Mark Pickhaver 78, 102, 103, 104
Frank Piper 3, 10, 11
Ian Polson 79
Anthony Possingham 77, 106, 108
Jane Powell 126, 127
Lindy Powell viii, 29, 54, 58, 59, 187
Daniel Praolini 84
Kelvyn Prescott 26, 67
Ian Press 254
Graham Prior 150, 216
Privy Council 104
Maurine Pyke 102, 218, 104, 218,

Q

David Quick 23, 61, 62, 64, 117, 164, 196
Peter Quinn 92

R

John Rau 91, 259
Rose-Marie Read 113
Rosie Read 126
Angus J Redford 126, 127
Geoffrey Reed 9, 10, 11, 18
William Retalic 77, 106, 108
Mark Rice 77, 86, 89
Paul Rice 86, 89, 205
Phillip Rice 54
Thomas Rice 135
Ross Richards 83, 97, 85
Sean Richter 97, 100, 106
David Riggall 109
Rohan Rivett 13, 103
Ian Roberts 126
Brendon Roberts 55, 256
Mark Roberts 92
Ian Robertson viii, 54, 58, 59, 68, 73, 233
Malcolm Robertson 67, 73, 171
James Robinson 154
Neville Rochow 86, 89, 117, 118, 119, 120, 231
Michael Roder 117, 232
Stephen Roder 117
Paul Rofe 126, 127, 182
Rose Park Chambers 76, 77, 78, 103, 157
Bruce Ross 11, 150
Margaret Ross 83, 116
Richard Ross-Smith 109, 112
Rumpole 26, 70, 71
Anthony Russell 53, 154

S

Michael Saies 106, 108
Robert Sallis 126
Roger Sallis 48, 79, 82, , 115
Christine Salvemini 72
Ian Sampson 113, 114
Keith (A K) Sangster 12, 21, 22, 53, 56, 57, 214
Philip Saunders 126
Trish Sced 72
Anthony Schapel 87, 90
Andrew Schatz 92
Selby Street Chambers 134
Bradley Selway 189
Separate bar 35, 36, 37, 39, 42
Shakespeare Chambers 74
Marie Shaw viii, 29, 76, 77, 78, 86, 194
Elizabeth Shepphard 122
Anne Sibree 134
Andrea Simpson 67, 73
Denys Simpson 117, 91, 119, 94
Sir Mellis Napier Chambers 121, 157, 202
Paul Slattery 109, 112, 213
Geoffrey Smart 74
C Villeneuve Smith 11
Cheryl Smith 80
David Smith 67, 73, 199
Frank Villeneuve Smith 9
Dorothy Christine Somerville 28
Rauf Soulio 91, 95
South Australian Bar Association 3, 15, 21, 35, 41, 44
Shane Spence viii, 92, 106, 276
Holly Stanley 88
Timothy Stanley 61, 64, 65, 227
Greg Stevens viii, 126, 127, 128
Kirsty Stewart 118
David Stokes 113
Randolph Stow 7
Francis Stratford 68
Edward Stratton-Smith 88, 90
Simon Stretton 48, 76, 77, 106, 107, 108, 235
Steven Strickland 83, 84, 200
John McDouall Stuart 93
Stuart Affair 13, 19
John Sulan viii, 25, 54, 59, 179
Chris Sumner 33, 34, 39, 40, 41, 42, 44, 57
Christopher Swan 106
Nicholas Swan 68, 79, 81, 82
Nicole Symons 91

T

Mark Taylor 88
Emily Telfer 131, 262

James Telfer 77, 106
Ian Thomas 55, 88, 118
Steven Thomas 117
Michael Tilley 107, 135
Sydney Tilmouth viii, 23, 53, 86, 88, 118, 176
Holly Tinning (see Leeson)
Andrew Tokley viii, 80, 81, 109, 246
Colonel Robert Torrens 81
Sir Robert Richard Torrens 80
Torrens Chambers 79, 80, 81, 82, 193
Paul Tothill 122, 123
Kym Tredrea 117
Darrell Trim 79, 80, 81, 82, 92, 193

U

Sam Ure

V

Ann Vanstone 111, 113, 114, 190
Holly Veale 68, 73
Victoria Chambers 48, 115
Victoria Square Chambers 133

W

Michael Wait 264
Kathryn Waite 88
Gillian Walker 92
Bernard Walrut 92
Stephen Walsh 86, 90, 181
Terry Walsh 15, 17
Michael Walter 216
Michael Ward 87
Robert Ward 57
Robert Wardell 6, 32
Sir Samuel Way 8, 22
P N Waye 157
W A Wearing 7
Wellington Chambers 47, 48, 49, 76, 163, 191
Anna Wells 62
Andrew Wells 11, 22, 57, 178
Jonathon Noye Wells viii, 61, 62, 64, 66, 178
William Wentworth 6, 7, 32
Vickianne West viii, 129
Ian White 113, 131
J M White 156
John White 107
Michael White 57, 153
Richard White 61, 64, 196
Dick Whitington 61, 64, 65, 192
David Whittle 78, 121
John Wickham 15, 23
David Wicks 25, 109, 110, 112, 183
Lloyd Wicks 55
Ivy Williams 27
Tim Williams viii, 54, 145, 276
Robert Williams 62
Nigel Wilson 42, 54, 58, 59
Sir Albert Wolff 23
Terence (Terry) Worthington 67, 73, 215
Wright Chambers 122

Y

Matthew Young 80

Z

Howard (H E) Zelling 3, 14, 15, 17, 21, 22, 47, 56, 57, 118, 119, 160, 164, 201, 202
Sesca Zelling 17, 28, 56

www.ingramcontent.com/pod-product-compliance
Ingram Content Group UK Ltd.
Pitfield, Milton Keynes, MK11 3LW, UK
UKHW062000041026
15591UKWH00016B/1096

9 780645 005615